Dedicated to my two brothers Donald "Duck" and Van "The Man" had not it been for them I would not have become the Hustler I became

## BOSTON

The early morning sun was rising in the blue November New England winter morning sky. It was time for me to get up and Massachusetts is just one of six states making up what is known as New England; however, of all its cities Boston is the city most people refer to. Massachusetts is recognized for many reasons, such as its historical past as well as various attractions. There are also the elite sports teams in every aspect of the sports world that represent the city of Boston.

There's the Boston Bruins, an amazing hockey team, there's the Celtics franchise that throughout their existence in the NBA has won over seventeen NBA Championships most of any team ever. The Boston Red Sox are one of the most exciting teams in major league baseball with a fan base that goes beyond Boston collectively known as "Red Sox Nation." Then there's the New England Patriots, an NFL team that's either loved or hated, but either way in the 21st century they have appeared in ten Super Bowls winning 6 Lombardi trophies, thus earning being recognized as one of the greatest teams in the NFL with the prestigious title "Dynasty."

Boston is a cultural melting pot renowned for its cutting-edge health care, technological advances, and world class education. Sought out by many well off eager high school graduates from all over the globe, in pursuit of the best education money can buy. Boston schools are the real upper echelon institutions, such as Harvard, M.I.T., and Boston University just to name a few. However, as for me before I became known as the WOLF in the game, neither of said mentioned reasons was why I ended up in Massachusetts.

# Origins

My journey began years ago from when I was a young boy living with family in Long Island N.Y. It was Long Island where I cracked my two front teeth trying to get away on my gold Schwinn bicycle ,which I had dubbed "The Getaway Bike". When I hit a trouble area in the street the front tire came rolling off. Maaaan, I went flying clean over the front handlebars. I was just trying to steal a bag of white powdered donuts. But even after the accident it didn't stop me from being the prolific hustler that I became. Even with what I consider my $50 smile.

However, it wasn't until my father moved the family from Long Island New York to St. Petersburg, Florida that I went from being just a common thief to becoming a hustler in the game. It was mainly due to a fallout that my father and I had, which resulted in me having to move out from his house and going to live with my two older brothers Donald "Duck" and Van "The Man".

I had no other choice. I had no real work skills at that time, so I had to resort to what I knew and considered my best talents, that was grifting. I did that in order to make it on my own. That was also how I justified it, so I didn't consider what I had to do as being wrong. As the years went by hustling was just like every other profession eventually, I leveled up found I had a special gift for grifting.

I became something a Jedi master with the hustling. I did it all with that $50 smile. Much Like in the business world. when you do great and raise to the top of your chosen profession, I became a CEO in the game of hustling.

My mother was part Italian the majority of her family lived in Chicago. My father was from the Carolinas and would often say that he was a black Frenchman. I don't know how they got to be living in New York, but that was where I was born in 1957.

It was 1960 something in the location Long Island, New York. I was single digits old constantly getting into mischief in grade school for either stealing, disrespecting teachers, or playing hooky. When I wasn't in school, I was stealing all sorts of items from the local neighborhood stores. So, by the time the family moved from New York to Florida I was set in my behavior.

However, I did have a slight thought about changing my ways, but that's about all it amounted to, just a passing thought. It didn't faze me not one iota. Stealing was the one thing that gave me a sense of accomplishment and recognition. Adoration was something I was always trying to receive from my older brothers, who applauded and commended me on my magician like skills, ninja quick reflexes, chess master like thinking. I did get busted several times during my younger years always for stealing and was sent to a juvenile detention center. I believe on my 3rd visit I was sent to Arthur G. Dozier School for Boys not once, but twice. But every time I was released, I went right back to grifting.

As my years went by and I became a teenager my misbehaving self-resulted and basically left me out on my own living with Don and Van. So, for me stealing became more than just something that I did for kicks and clout. It became my way of surviving. It was my profession.

I began hustling downtown St. Petersburg infiltrating my way around and into the jeweler's world. I was stealing and dealing in diamonds, rubies, sapphires, emeralds, gold, silver and platinum, along with gold, and silver coins from countless jewelry stores and coin shops. I'd say from the age of 15 through 19 I had to have stolen no less than $250,000 in said items. If life had a reflection effect, I believe that I would have made those business owners very unhappy with the unrecoverable financial lost I had caused them. So, I was not allowed to live in St. Petersburg. When I did finally get caught years into the game at the age of 18 and was sent away to Florida state prison on a two-year sentence. When I got out, I had to leave St. Petersburg, Florida.

It was 1980 something when I was released from Florida state prison. My mother picked me up at the bus station and on the way to the house she told me there was something she needed to talk to me about.

After dinner she approached me and informed me, without telling me who said it. Due to my past criminal endeavors, I was no longer welcome at that time in the city of St. Petersburg. My mother had made arrangements for me to move from St. Petersburg, Florida to go live with my grandmother and father in Brookline, Massachusetts. It's a suburban area of Boston and that is how I ended up in Boston.

It was a challenge for me in the early stage of living in the city. I tried to work different jobs, but the pay never seemed to satisfy my financial needs, so in order to live in the city the way I wanted to, I knew I had another skill that in the pass was very profitable. That skill was grifting and so I reawakened the spirit of the Wolf. The city hustling life required more of that skill, so I expanded on my hustling ability to the maximum level becoming something like a Jedi master in the art of grifting. And in doing so I created the persona THE WOLF, a serious no jive MUTHAFUCKAN HUSTLER. In. doing so earning me the utmost respect, adoration, and recognition amongst my peers. The most well-known of hustlers in the game and all over. I was that dude and one smooth muthafucka for sure.

These events are absolutely the truth, but if at times they seem repetitive it's because with so much similarity in my adventures it's impossible for me to get things respectively in chronologically order. But every hustle I mention is true, just as I was true to the game. So, allow my words in this book to take you to places and events that maybe you have or have not heard of or experienced.

This venture isn't another story about gang banging, shooting, or killing. It's not another lame story about selling drugs. This is a high-class venture into the life of a hustler who stole and dealt in diamonds, platinum, gold, sapphires and rubies. I was able to bypass all sorts of security, manipulating my way into an assortment of complexes, hospitals, colleges and businesses. Wear uniforms and donning numerous types of attire. I was a businessman, a lawyer, and a professor just to mention a few. I was always able to stay in character. I'll take you from the southern ghetto streets of St. Petersburg, Florida to the meanest streets of Boston, Massachusetts and other states.

# Twice New York once Florida

When I was five years old my father moved the family from Brooklyn, New York to Long Island, New York and when I was eight, he moved the family to St. Petersburg, Florida. As far back as I can remember I got into all kinds of mischief. My behavior caused my father and I to have a rocky relationship. I was often the recipient of a belt beating, but there were times when not only did I get the belt, but my punishment would be that I had to spend the weekend in a room in the basement. I was not allowed to go outside to play, and I didn't get anything to eat.

My delinquent behavior resulted in me getting sent to Arthur G. Dozier, a reformatory school for boys. I was no older than eight when I was sent there for the first time, fourteen the second time, and I was fifteen when I got released. After all that, my thinking was the same as when I went in. Thus, causing my father and I to get into a serious almost fight. It was that day that I knew even without my father saying a word to me that it was time for me to leave his home.  So, I did, I ended up going to my two older brothers' cottage to live.

This is what led to that day. My father was practicing the religion Jehovah Witness in accordance with the teaching there were certain rules or behavior that had to be followed. My father expected all that were living under his roof to adhere to that. However, I was carrying on and living my life not in accordance with my father's expectations. I was what was called a worldly person. I was stealing, getting into trouble and hanging out in the streets with friends drinking alcohol and smoking weed. Often returning to the house not only way past the expected hour that my father set, but I would either be drunk, high or both.

It was a Thursday night, like every other Thursday night it was the eighteen and under dance party at Campbell Park recreation center located on 16th Street. It was another warm Florida sun shining day. I was up early in the morning, washed myself headed into town to go get my hustle on. I made a few stings here and there by noon I had enough money to service my needs for Thursday.

On my way back to the house I bought a nickel bag of weed, rolled and smoked a joint, then stopped in at the Piggly Wiggly got some snacks a strawberry soda then made my way home. It was still early so I spent my time in my bedroom listing to some fly tunes, then selected what I was going to wear to the dance: a pair of bell bottoms pants, a wide collar button down shirt with the wide puffy sleeves, along with a pair of black platform shoes.

After listing to music for several hours I took a nap. By the time I awakened it was five p.m. I went to the kitchen and got something to eat and by seven I went to the bathroom to take a shower. Ten or fifteen minutes later I was back in my room drying off. I applied the necessary male cosmetics before getting dressed, picked out my afro sprayed it with afro sheen.

I pocketed my cash along with my bag of weed and headed out the door. I was ready for another evening of partying if my skills have it hopefully, I'll get some pussy. I stepped out of the house into the warm Florida air accompanied by a slight breeze. It was the 70's the atmosphere was cool, calm and collective.

I felt good I did my best pimp walk down the avenues and streets on my way to the dance at Campbell Park center. I could hear the sound of the music of the 70's playing from inside the center as I approached the building.  But more important were the beautiful sexy young hood flowers emanating outside heading into the building. I made my way to the back of the center to get my head right. I knew some of the fellas that would be hanging out smoking weed drinking Boones Farms strawberry hill wine.

We did the traditional 70s soul brother greeting followed by an "aye what's happening man". I reached into my pocket pulled out my nickel bag of weed rolled up a joint. After placing the bag back into my pocket, I looked around for a light. Someone in the group passed me a lighter I lit up the joint. I took a couple of pulls before passing it to one of the fellas. Someone produced another bottle of Boones Farm we smoked the herb, while drinking the wine before going into the venue. Indulging in general conversation while over exaggerating our past accomplishment to some of the young female hood flowers would be considered spiting pregame back then. I was lit and ready to party, so I left the group made my way into the Center. The atmosphere was nice, the lights were low the funky music was playing a smooth groove, all of which placed me in the right mood. I was ready to mingle. I made my way around the place using my wolf senses like I was casing a joint. Only I was profiling these tender red bones there was so many to choose from. From a short distance I saw her. I walked over to where she was. "Say girl, what's up?" I said.

"Not much," she said.

"Well, since there's nothing going on right now for neither one of us let's make it happen. Do you want to dance?" I asked. She said "yes" so we made our way to the dance floor. I watched Soul Train every Saturday, so I knew how to dance, she was also an excellent dancer. After dancing to several fast songs, I grabbed her hand to escorted her off the dance floor. I asked her to go with me to a quiet area away from the loud music but close enough to still hear the music. But it was just low enough for me to have a conversation with her.

"What's your name and sign?" I asked her.

"Jackie," she said, "and I'm a Scorpio."

However, no matter what she said her sign was I was going to convince her that she and I were compatible. "Solid," I said. "I'm a Pisces."

All throughout our conversation I kept my ears turned to the music as it was being played and then I heard what I had been waiting for a slow jam! This was my opportunity to get her out on the dance floor to get my grind on.

"Say girl, let's dance." She went with me to the floor I held her close to my body, we danced with our bodies close to one another ever so slowly griding dragging dat ass. I dipped and swayed with every movement. Hoping to be giving her a taste of what it could be like under the sheets with me. She didn't resist as a matter of fact she treated me to my imagination. As the song was coming to an end I popped the question.

"So, Jackie, what are you doing after the dance?"

"Nothing." she said.

"Can I walk you home tonight after the dance?
You see, me spending time with you would be not only for me. But a chance for you and I to get to know one another."

"Okay," she said we danced to a couple more songs than one more slow jam. The lights began coming on one after the other we knew what that meant, the dance was coming to an end. The night air was warm as we walked to her house.

"Do you smoke weed?" I asked her.

"Sure," she said so I lit up a joint then put my arm around her. As we smoked, we walked and talked about her. I was laying my best Mack game on her it seemed to have worked. When we arrived at her house, we went up into the Florida porch, which was enclosed surrounded by a screen. She asked me to sit on the couch to wait for her, telling me that she'll be out to join me in a few minutes.

I sat down on the couch waiting contemplating what was next. When Jackie returned, she was wearing a pair of hot pants (cutoff jeans) long with a tee shirt. I could tell from the way her titties were moving under her T- shirt that she didn't have a bra on. She sat next to me and informed me that her parents were home inside their bedroom down the hall watching TV.

We talked a little more then I made my move. I started French kissing her and she returned the passion. I tasted the sweetness of her mouth as my tongue ventured within her mouth, I could feel the warmth coming from her body. It was southern quiet outside, with a warm cool atmosphere. I laid her back onto the couch, lifted her T-shirt began sucking on her erect nipples, while at the same time unbuttoning the button on her hot pants. My hand slowly making its way down her front until I reached the warmth of the inside of her pussy. I began rubbing her clit with my middle finger her pussy became wet. The thought of what was coming made my dick hard as Chinese arithmetic.

I kissed her on her neck, making my way down under her shirt to her nipples, each one erected I sucked on each one after the other. I felt her hand as she found her way to my pants. She unzipped my pants releasing my hard dick, I pulled her hot pants down over one of her legs. I climbed on top of her. Her pussy was warm tight and wet. We began fucking yet knowing that we had to keep the passion noise as low as possible so as to not let her parents hear us. She let out a moan it was over as I busted my load inside of her. I pulled my pants back up as she pulled up her hot pants.

We sat on the couch talked for a few minutes. I said good night then made my way home. By the time I got there it had to be close to midnight, maybe later. There were no lights on inside of the house. Placing my key inside the lock I unlocked the front door stepping into the darkness of the house then BAM!

My father was waiting in the darkness for me to return. The sound of his voice engulfed the room startling me. He said, "son you can't continue coming into my house the way you have been late at night intoxicated." I heard his voice, however, what he said went in one ear then right out the other. I was buzzing off the weed and the booze. I went to my room and feel asleep.

The following day I woke up to the warmth of the Florida sun shining through my bedroom window upon my skin. I didn't know what time it was. I was still in the slumber of last night, but I was thirsty and hungry. I felt the warmth of the floor under my feet as I climbed out of bed making my way down the hallway to the bathroom to wash my face. From there I went to the kitchen to address my hunger and thirst.

Sitting at the table in the kitchen was my father drinking a cup of coffee. When I walked in he addressed me. I could hear the seriousness in his voice when he said, "Son you have been coming into my house on your own free will disregarding what I expect of you. I am no longer going to tolerate you disrespecting me and my house. Then the final statement was "There can only be one man under this roof that man is me"!

Me being young swollen up with pride, I responded inappropriately, an argument ensued that spilled out into the backyard. Things were getting heated and tense I knew what I had to do. My father didn't have to say another word. It was time for me to leave. I hopped over the backyard fence running off.

There was only one place that I knew I could go. The Florida air was warm so by the time I arrived at my brothers' place sweat was running down my face and back. The sound of soulful music was emanating from inside the cottage. I stood outside of the front door waiting until I caught my breath. I knocked once, but there was no answer it would take several attempts until my brother Van opened the door. From the look in his eyes, I could see that he was loaded.

"Say little bro, what's up?" he asked. The smell of weed after smoke was permeating from inside the cottages exiting out dissipating into the sky. I explained to him what had transpired between father and I he invited me in. From that day until I was able to get my own place that was home. It was the perfect setting as far as I was concerned as both of my brothers lived a lifestyle in sync with how I wanted to live, so everything was cope esthetic.

# Out the House

My brothers Van and Don made their money in the drug game, so the majority of their time was spent out in the streets and at "The Three Oaks." That left me at the cottage by myself most of the time left to my own vices. When I was out and about in the streets, we would often meet up at a designated place to check in on one another. I needed a regular source of income. I wasn't skilled in any kind of profession and didn't even complete junior high school, so my brother Van attempted to assist me with my dilemma. He would give me a dope sack which consisted of twenty packages of heroin. Each package of dope was $20 which netted $400. My cut was $100. I sold drugs for a few months, but it wasn't my forte. I was a thief and more comfortable with that form of getting money, so I returned back to what I did best and that was the take fast, but I had to step up my hustle no more junior hustling. I was going to contribute to the household and carry my weight.

I remember the first time I stole jewelry and sold it. The money that I received made me realize it was well worth the effort. So, I mainly focused my attention and skills on stealing those kinds of items. It was a learning process and required some serious creativity to go into jewelry stores and coin shops. I really had to finesse and manipulate my way around. After all we are talking about stealing and getting away with gold, diamonds, sapphires, precious stones, and antique coins.

But in doing so my income was exceeding the normal standards and I was pulling my weight and much more. When I began learning and retaining the knowledge of the jeweler's world. I was able to deal and trade at top dollar for what I was selling. So, by the time I got to Boston I was well versed and full of knowledge in the field of gemology and jewelry.

I, like most hustlers in the life get caught up in some form of addiction and for me it was cocaine. I went from weed and liquor to heroin and settled on cocaine. Which during my time in the game was considered the rich man's high, I used cocaine in every form possible. My cocaine habit took me on a venture into places I never dreamed or thought I would go or be. Just as I was locked into the fast money of the hustler game, cocaine tagged along for the ride.

# Out into the world

It was not just another sunny day, this was the day I was to be released from Florida state prison after serving two years I was more than ready to leave. I was twenty-two years young and in excellent shape. I packed up my personal belongings, took a shower, dressed and headed to the reception office after changing into my street clothing. I signed my release paper and was given a hundred dollars, and a bus ticket to my destination complimentary of the state of Florida. I was driven to the Greyhound bus station by one of the prison guards where I was left to wait for my bus. I felt the goodness of my freedom and the view of the people, but mainly most if not every female at the bus station as they attended to their business. The sound of the announcer voice came over the intercom awakened me from my daydreaming thoughts, "Bus to Tampa, St. Petersburg."

I boarded the bus with the other passengers and went to the back of the bus and sat down. The sound of the people on the bus was a welcoming sound. I spent most of my time enjoying the scenery that passed by on my way home. The bus made several stops along the way. Then I was back in St. Petersburg as the bus driver announced my stop over the bus speaker. I grabbed what little property I had and stepped off the bus and walked into the waiting area. I saw my mother and older sister Lynn waiting with smiles on their faces. Hugs and kisses and happy to see you were exchanged.

I followed them to the car, a four-door white Lincoln continental mother started the car and drove into the traffic. During the conversation between my mother and I as she was driving to the house, she said to me that there was something important that she needed to talk to me about in private. The car pulled up in the driveway to the house. I was so glad to be home. We all got out of the car and went inside the house. I went to put away my things in the side room of the front Florida room, grabbed a change of clothing and a towel and went to the bathroom. I took a shower, changed into something more suitable and went to the kitchen where my mother was preparing dinner. She was busy so I went to the living room and watched TV until dinner was ready.

Fifteen minutes later my mother called me into the kitchen; it was time to have that talk. Without revealing anyone in particular my mother informed me that due to my past hustling escapades throughout downtown St. Petersburg, people were not happy and had advised her that I was no longer welcome in the city. WOW I thought. My mother knowing that beforehand had made arrangement for me to move to the state of Massachusetts to go live with her side of the family with my grandparent's.

Two days later at the young age of twenty-one I was on the Greyhound bus with a ticket from St. Petersburg, Florida to Boston, Massachusetts, the big city. I had no idea of what it would be like or what to expect. I knew nothing about Boston culture nor its lifestyle. What I did bring with me was my experience and versatility of hustling in the streets at a very young age, as well as years spent in not only in school, but in state prison as well. It was either do or die, win or lose and I had always been in it to win it. I started out playing my game day by day close to the cement and off the bricks."

# My Past My Future

It was late evening and the afternoon sun had faded away into the background of the evening Florida sky. I felt the vibration of the bus tires on the road up through the bottom of my body in my seat. The Greyhound bus continued moving down the highway taking me further away from Florida and closer and closer to the city of Boston a.k.a "The Bean". I was a 22-year-old black man with a street education, very little work experience and $100 in my pocket. I had a couple of incidents along the way, nothing major, but I dealt with it appropriately. I don't remember the day I arrived in Boston, but it was early 7 maybe 8 am. As the bus made its way through the city, not only did I feel the difference from the atmosphere. The look of the city was big and tall buildings from eye to eye and hundreds of pedestrians like ants moving here and there.

The Greyhound bus pulled into what I believe was South station. I had picked up a situation along the way a young white girl. A runaway looking for life other than the one that she was running from, so l used that little information to my advantage promising her that when she and I got to Boston she could stay with me. That was a lie, I used her femininity to help me hustle this guy who was a passenger on the bus.

I had her all wrapped up in my game before he got on the bus, however, I noticed he was interested in her and started bragging to her. She told me that he told her he had a large bag of weed, and a couple thousands of dollars, she also found out he kept in an arm duffle bag he had. So, I put her to work based on the fact that when the bus made stops for chow the dude would bring her back something to eat on his dime. I knew that he had an emotional attachment and was looking for some afternoon delight.

When I was able to talk to her without him noticing, I gave her instructions that we needed to get that money for our future. I told her I needed for her to wait until night and get him into the bus bathroom. So, when the bus made a stop for dinner at a one of those big truck stops, I went inside and grabbed a plastic sandwich sized bag and kept it in my pocket for the planned moment that I had made with her.

After dinner all the passengers returned to the bus and sat down to settle in for the night. As the bus proceeded down the highway, she sat with him, and I waited for the late night grift. The time arrived and I laid back in my seat like every other passenger, but I wasn't asleep. I was watching the girl and the guy from the slits of my eyes. Moments later I watched as the two of them got up from their seats and made their way to the bathroom.

When I heard the door close and lock, I went into action in the darkness of the bus. I crept down the aisle to where he was sitting, and I began searching his only bag. It didn't take me long to find what I was looking for his stash of marijuana and the cash. I took the money first and then took the plastic bag out of my pocket and filled it with a large amount of marijuana. I went back to my set and acted as if I was asleep.

Sometime later he and her returned from the bathroom and sat down and she entertained him for a while with conversation. During the ride to his destination, he didn't take a look into his duffle bag I was relieved when he got off the bus at his destination. The bus pulled into my destination hours later and the girl and I exited the bus together and walked into the bus station terminal. I needed to separate myself from her. I asked her to sit down in one of the chairs in the terminal and wait whiles I make a call to my friend, to let him know that I'm in Boston with a friend and he needs to come pick us up, she smiled at that comment.

I left her sitting in the chair and went to locate a pay phone making sure that I got as far away from her as possible without her noticing what I was doing. I located a pay phone and dropped coins in the slot I dialed the number that my mother gave me. I listened as the phone rung once, twice and on the third ring my grandmother answered. "Hello" the voice said.

"Hi grandma, this is your grandson where's G-Pa?"

"He should be outside the station somewhere waiting for you. Look for a dark green Buick 225," she said. "Thanks," I said and hung up the receiver. I walked back over to where I had left the white girl. She was still sitting in the chair waiting. I made my way to one of the many doors and stepped outside. I looked to my left and then to my right and I saw the dark green Buick 225 parked at the curb amongst other cars idling. I walked over to the car and knocked on the window. The car window went down and a man in his late 60's was behind the wheel. I asked him, "are you Willie?" He said yes and I said, "It's me your grandson."

"Hello," he said, "get into the car." I opened up the door, got in and closed it. He pulled away and into the Boston city traffic. I gave no thought or consideration of the white girl that I had left behind at the bus station leaving her to her on devices and in search of her dreams. Thoughts occupied my mind as we drove in silence. I admired the city landscape of tall buildings and the congestion of people moving about in different directions to their destinations. For some reason I felt at home.

# Brookline Massachusetts

"Here we are," G-Pa said to me as he was parking his duce and a quarter Buick in front of the apartment building where he was living with my grandmother. This would be my temporary place of residence, the town of Brookline, which at that time was just one of Massachusetts many up-scale communities. This was the beginning of my life in Boston.

My G- Pa had a job lined up for me at the Getty's gas station where he was also working. My hours were 11 pm till 7 A.M. The station was right up the street from where we were living. I worked there no more than four months, I just wasn't able to work around so much temptation such as handling the station money, knowing where the safe was located and knowing that it was kept unlocked during working hours. Plus working eight plus hours a day, five six days a week just to get paid one day out of the week, and after the government took theirs there wasn't much for me to enjoy life.

I knew that I was capable of making more money without anyone giving a dime to no one. The soul of the hustler in me made a few quick bucks hustling items and other flim-flams that I came up with at the gas station. That was small cash, and my paycheck wasn't enough to fulfill the needs required for the city and self-satisfaction. It was inevitable for me to return back to the game of hustling.

# BACK IN THE GAME

The early morning October New England sky was blue, and the air was as crisp as a bag of Lays potato chips. Today was the day I planned to venture out of my small, encircled environment I had been living in. Since the day I had arrived, I had wanted to explore the city around me. It would begin in the town of Brookline. I grabbed a bath towel from the pile of towels in the closet and made my way to the bathroom. I stepped into the shower and let the lukewarm water hit my face awakening me completely.

Five minutes later I stepped out of the shower, dried off and headed back to my small bedroom. I put on a pair of dress slacks and shirt and tie. I slipped into a pair of comfortable shoes for the journey I was about to take. I donned a black overcoat to keep the New England chill off me. I splashed on some cologne and headed quietly out the door to not awaken my grandparents. I walked at my own pace amongst the pedestrians on the sidewalk. The traffic was light as people made their way to their prospective destinations. As I walked making my way into the town I was looking and waiting for the opportunity that awaited me. I continued my way up Brookline Avenue heading towards Brookline Village and then I felt it. I knew what it was. It was the feeling that I have always felt like so many times while hustling in Florida.

I knew that somewhere opportunity was in close proximity, and I decided that it had to be in one of the many buildings. I entered one of those building and the lobby was void of any personnel or security guards and the only sound was the sound of the building. There were a few lights turned on just enough to cast my shadow upon the walls. As it followed me as I slowly made my way up two flights of stairs.

I walked down the corridor trying door after doors hoping to find one unlocked, but each one was locked. Finally, I came upon one that was unlocked. I turned the handle and opened the door slowly and cautiously making sure to make as little noise as possible. It was a large open space floor office. I glanced around looking to see if anyone was around. I didn't see a single worker, and there was no one at any of the many desks that occupied the office.

I entered with awareness, I went from to desk to desk checking each and every drawer. There was nothing of value worth taking. I noticed a large, enclosed office to itself, I knew this had to be the office of someone in charge. I quickly made my way over to the office, went in and began checking the drawers. Nothing special worth taking until something caught my eye! To the upper right-hand corner on top of the desk I saw a bulging white envelope, the kind with the plastic window on the front. I couldn't believe what I was seeing, it was an envelope filled with paper money.

I grabbed the envelope and quickly exited the office down the stairs and out of the building into the hustling and bustling of the town of Brookline. The morning sun seemed to be much brighter to me now that I had gotten away with an envelope full of money. I did my best to get as far away from the building and that area. The sound of my footsteps on the sidewalk was all that I heard I walked until I came upon what was a small inside mall. Perfect I thought. I entered and blended in with the flow of the morning workers and people. I looked around for the men's room after locating it, I ducked inside one of stalls closed, and locked the door behind me.

I sat down on the toilet seat and pulled the envelope from out of my pocket and began counting the money. Most of the bills were $20s, ten or more were $100s and $50s and there were $10s and $5s as well. I smiled. The cash felt like a beautiful lady in my hands. The final tally was a little over $3,000. I pocketed the large bills in one pocket and the rest in the other, tore up the envelope and discarded it in the toilet bowl. The sound of the toilet flushing was the only sound I heard as I exited the men's room.

With over three thousand dollars in my possession there was no need for me to continue hustling. The emptiness in my stomach required attention and it was time for breakfast. I made my way down the streets filled with people in search of a place to eat. Along the way I made mental pictures of the town, its citizens, its public stores and all its shops. There were numerous opportunities that I saw along the way just waiting to be plucked by me at another time.

I was famished. I stopped at one of Brookline's finest restaurants for breakfast. I walked in the restaurant and a beautiful waitress welcomed me. On top of the counter was a copy of the Boston Globe. I picked it up and carried it with me. As she escorted me to my seat, she gave me a menu and then asked, "Would you like some coffee sir?"

"Yes." I said and she poured coffee from a silver pot into a China coffee cup, smiled and walked away. She returned a few minutes later which gave me enough time to view the menu. After refilling my cup, she asked if I was ready to order. "Yes," I said, "I'll have a glass of orange juice, three eggs scrambled soft with some shredded cheddar on top, three link sausages and wheat toast please." She walked away to place my order.

I opened the Boston Globe and read the articles of the day, enjoying what had to be gourmet coffee. In no time my breakfast arrived. Breakfast with endless coffee was delicious from the beaning to its end. I left a healthy tip along with the price of the meal on the table before exiting the restaurant.

As I made my way back home, I thought about my experiences and understood what it meant to be someone of means living life as a Bostonian. From that one experience I made a commitment to myself that from that day forward. I was going to do whatever I had to do to make sure that I'd maintain that form of lifestyle. I was hustling whenever I could throughout Brookline and was making enough money to enjoy the lifestyle that I had committed to myself.

Brookline was a town and there was only so much hustling that could be done. so, as time went by I was extending my ground hustle further away from Brookline closer, and closer into the city of Boston. Days became months, months turned into years, and with ever accomplishment I was adapting to the hustle and bustle of the city, learning and becoming more and more a Bostonian, bettering my skill in the game of the grifting.

# THE LAB

The early morning sun was rising in the blue November
New England winter morning sky. It was time for me to get up and
get ready for work, my title **HUSTLER**. I got out of the comfort of
my warm bed and felt the cold air of the room. I was awake shook
the sleep off and walked barefoot to the bathroom to relive myself. I
turned on the shower, stepped in to awaken myself. Afterwards I
made my way back to the bedroom drying myself off with a bath
towel along the way.

I selected my attire for today, tannish brown dress slacks,
white shirt with a power tie, and a pair of dark brown easy walking
dress shoes. I was dressed to handle any situation that I would
come upon. My overcoat was light brown camel hair. I stepped
outside into the cold Boston winter's morning, every breath that I
took, every exhale combined with the warmth of my breath
delivered a cool cloud into the air.

I went into a hustler's mood. I had a regiment that I always
followed. First and foremost, I didn't eat. The hunger that I felt in
my stomach would be the fuel that motivated me. The holidays
"Thanksgiving and Christmas" were approaching. Children of all
ages were walking making their way to their perspective schools as
their parents made their way to their way to their perspective jobs
or back home.

I pressed the automatic starter on my key chain as I walked to my car the engine of my four-door white Lincoln Continental roared to life. I unlocked the door sat on the driver's side, buckled up the seat belt, put the car in drive and pulled out of the parking lot into the traffic with no particular heading. I'd let my hustler intuition guide me.

I drove past schools, businesses, houses with nothing capturing my hustler intuition. I kept driving looking along the way in different directions until I noticed a large brick building down in the woods, off the path of the main road. I could feel it, this was the place. I turned down the dirt road, drove to the back of the building, parked in the parking lot and turned off the motor.

It was still early in the morning and had to be seven no later than eight. I got out of the car, removed my overcoat put it in the back seat. Checked my appearance, I was ready. I walked towards the back of the building and located the delivery entrance. I climbed up the metal stairs and turned the handle of the door. It was unmuthafucking unlocked!

I looked in and around there was no one on the dock. I walked through the delivery area into the employees' part of the building. Slowly, but cautiously I walked down one side of what was a two-sided corridor going into offices one after the other. I didn't find what I was looking for and ended up at the opposite end of the corridor where steps lead down to what I could see was a cafeteria type of lounge area for the employees. they were all involved in conversations socializing, drinking coffee, or enjoying breakfast. I wasn't there for breakfast.

To the opposite side of me was what appeared to be a laboratory? There were no more than three employees dressed in white lab coats attending to whatever business was at their beckon, which kept them preoccupied. I cautiously walked pass the window and no one noticed me. I continued my hustler down the other side of the corridor always keeping a watchful eye out, but the coast remained clear.

I went into unoccupied office after office, looking behind desks and doors for a lady's purse, or any men's jackets. I keep hustling, moving cautiously like a Wolfs ears in tuned to every sound that was around as my eyes kept scanning my surroundings.

Finally, I came upon what I was looking for, a purse left unattended behind a desk on the floor. I picked it up, looked inside removed the wallet and opened it up. There had to be seven possible more credit cards. I took two credit cards from behind the front cards. That was part of the grift that I had incorporated into my thinking. Knowing that if I take cards from the back leaving the view as the owner remembered it no one would be the wiser. I would always leave whatever money was in the wallet so as to not draw attention to what I did. Giving me as much time as I needed to use those credit cards taking cash would only set off an alarm.

I replaced the wallet back in the purse and placed it in the same location as I remembered. I repeated that process one more time. In one of the offices, I came upon a man's jacket on the back of the chair. I checked the inside pocket finding a billfold, I took two credit cards and replaced the billfold back in the jacket. It was time to get the hell out of there.

I had stolen six credit cards. I didn't go out the same way I entered. I left out the front entrance lobby seeing that there was no one sitting at the front desk entrance. I made my exit and to my car, started it and drove away. I drove to the Peabody malls. I was dressed like a businessman or a man of importance, who had pockets of knowledge and confidence.

All these factors would be helpful in me pulling off the use of the stolen credit cards without drawing suspicion to myself. I had perfected my game. I parked my car, put on my coat and headed inside the mall. I walked up and down the mall corridor looking for the right opportunity.

A Bay's jeweler's advertisement caught my attention. It was the holiday season, and they were having a special sale buy one item get the other item half off. From the outside window looking in I noticed that one of the employees was young. This would fit perfectly into my plan.

I walked into the store with confidence and went straight to her. "Good morning," I said.

"Good morning," she replied, "may I help you?"

"Yes," I said. "A long-term colleague and close friend of mine is relocating to New York to start up his own practice. I and the other affiliates wanted to get him something special in remembrance of his time with the team."

"Is there anything in particular that you had in mind? she asked.

"Yes," I said. "We've decided on getting him a gold I. D. bracelet."

"Good choice," she said.

She unlocked the jewelry case and pulled out a tray with an assortment of men's bracelets. I went into jeweler's mode of what knowledge I had of gold, incorporating that into the conversation hoping this would give me more clout as well as her trust. I know that most men's jeweler is 18kt. gold as to make it sturdier and the price of gold today is (I quoted the price of gold at that time, did a few calculations in comparison to what they were asking) thus telling her that it was a reasonable price.

She showed me a few bracelets, we went through the same process then I made my choice. I was ready to make the purchase, that's when she intervened and informed me that today there was a special. I could get another item at 50% off along the item I was buying. Okay I looked at a few items and then made my selection, a beautiful man's cluster diamond ring at $1,500, but at 50% off. She rung up the two items as $1,800.

"Will that be cash or credit, sir?" she asked.

"Credit," I responded

and handed her the platinum man's cards.

"Is it possible to get those in a gift box?" I asked.

"Sure," she said,

it was the icing on the cake. The card went through with no problem, and she didn't ask me for any form of I. D. I left the store with a smile and the bag of items. I waited until I was several stores away that's when I took the diamond ring out of the bag, removed it from the box put it on my finger and tossed the box. I felt a little more in character of the roles that I was performing as a businessman of means.

It was time to go on my usual shopping spree. I stopped at one of the venders within the mall to have the man's bracelet engraved with my last name in capital letters. After that I went on another one of my shopping sprees.

It was my intellectual hustler decision to rotate each card after each use, the purpose to that decision was not to draw the attention of unusual spending from the credit card company computer monitoring systems. That's why I would make sure I to steal no less than four cards every time I went out hustling. I had spent hours walking up and down the mall, in and out of stores, then back to my car with loads and loads of packages, tons of bags all from credit cards purchases, now I was famished. I made my last round to the car to put bags in the trunk, then went back in the mall to get something to eat. First

I went and picked up my gold bracelet. It was beautiful as the bold capital letters of my last name stood out **Boulders**. I paid cash for the work and put the bracelet on my wrist. It complimented the clustered diamond ring on my finger. There was a restaurant that I had noticed in the mall that I had planned on eating at "Joe's bar and grill." The place was busy, so I sat at the bar. The bar tender came over gave me a menu and asked, "Sir would you like something to drink?"

"Yes, I'll have a double shot of Hennessey and for an appetizer I will have the shrimp cocktail."
The bar tender left returned a few minutes later with my drink. Three minutes more he came back with my shrimp cocktail placed it before me.

"Are you ready to order sir?" he asked.

"Yes. I'll have the filet mignon medium rear with steak fries and a Caesar salad."

I watched the Celtics on the provided television as I enjoyed my Hennessey and appetizer. The bar tender returned ten minutes later with my meal. I did it big Willy style as I watched television and ate my steak with a double shot of Hennessey. I paid for my meal with one of the stolen credit cards, signed the slip and left. I had satisfied my hunger and it was time to get back to business.

I drove to Stop and Shop, a grocery store and did some grocery shopping. Selecting only brand name products and items, as well as choice cut steaks and meats. I shopped until my shopping cart was filled with all kinds of top shelf goodies. I would always look for a curtain type of cashier when it came time to selected one.

I got in line and when it was my time to check out, I made sure to flash my diamond ring as well as displaying my gold bracelet. I made casual conversation with the semi-elderly female cashier, as well as helping to bag the groceries. The cost of the groceries was over $200. I swiped one of the credit cards in my possession, pushed the necessary buttons and the card was approved.

I exited the store with a cart full of groceries and went to my car. After loading the bags in my car, I could see that there was no room in my car to fit anything else. On the way home I stopped at the Shell gas station on the Lynn way, which was usually the last stop I make before heading home. I filled my car tank with only the best gasoline high test and selected the most expensive car wash available.

I had not only spoiled myself, but everything else of mine and that included my Lincoln. I pulled out of the car wash and onto the Lynn way, turned on my car stereo and jammed all the way home. I pulled in front of the house, unloaded everything from the car into the house the car I parked on the side of the house, locked it and went back into the house to put everything away.

Twenty minutes later I was back in my car driving again to Union Street to one of my frequent hang outs Charlie Chan's, a Chinese food and bar. I had a lady friend that worked there her, and I would do a hustle with the credit cards.

"What's up Wolf?" I heard as I walked into the bar and sat at the bar. The question came from a familiar lady friend who was working behind the bar.

"You know what's up."

"Same thing?" she asked.

"Yep." She knew the deal. She would ring up a sale for $100 dollars, keep forty dollars and the rest was mine along with free drinks.

"Bacardi rum and coke with a twist of lime?" she asked.

"Yes," I said.

She did the deal, gave me my percentage and then I ordered a large poo-poo platter with an order of large shrimp fried rice. I made casual conversation with the one of the ladies sitting at the bar as I waited for the food. I excused myself with drink in hand, walked over to the juke box, put five dollars in the slot and selected songs, including several requests from other female patrons.

I returned back to the bar, sat down and a few minutes later the bar tender came with my order. I sat the food on top of the bar. "Can I get several plates and forks?" I asked her. When she returned, I asked if anyone wanted some Chinese food as music was playing from the jukebox. I made conversation with the lady behind the bar after consuming my drink.

From there I went next door to the phone store to talk with the owner who was one of my many clients, then returned home. I would make several returns back to that lab building and the results were always successful. However, I knew that in the game that I was playing everything must come to an end and so I discontinued going to the LAB.

# Becoming Dr. J. Eddie

It was the year 2000 something, during this time in my life I had met this lady she was a few years older than me of Cuban descent. We decided to live together at her apartment. On days that I went out hustling I noticed that there was a hospital and high school in close proximity to the apartment where we resided. I was up and ready the next morning sometime around 7 a.m. The high school was my target.

I felt the morning coolness upon my skin as I separated myself from the warmth of the naked body of my lady lying next to me in bed. She made a soft rustling sound as I untangled myself from her arms and slowly made my way to the shower turning the water on. I stepped into the shower grabbed the bar Duke Cannon soap from the soap dish and showed. I stepped out of the shower after drying myself I applied the necessary male cosmetics and began dressing.

I knew the image that I had to play; I put on black dress slacks a white Van Heusen dress shirt, Brooks Brothers Rep tie, and a pair of Bostonian shoes. I put on my diamond ring, with a gold watch, with just a splash but not too overbearing of DIOR cologne. I viewed my appearance in the mirror I was Professor J. Eddie

I kissed my lady on the forehead picked up my gold cross pen along with a pencil off the dresser, placed them in my shirt pocket and headed out the door. Pushing the button on the remote starter the engine to my Lincoln came to life. With another push of the button unlocked the car door I climbed in and drove out of the parking lot over to the high school. I parked in a location that was close enough but not far away yet easy to relocate. I was able to get into the school without incident. As I walked down the corridor, I greeted the students they were cordial back, most of the teachers were out of their classrooms doing their morning usual's. So, I took advantages of that dipping into the rooms, and swiping credit cards from out of wallets, and bags left in and under desks before they could return back to their classrooms.

Once I had three credit cards, I went shopping for all kinds of household items and ate lunch. I was a regular at the high school. Students, other teachers and staff thought I was a substitute professor. I would go hustling there at different times, yet still I had to change doing that my hustler's intuition told me things were getting hot.

I went to the hospital that was down the road. Pulled up opened the trunk of my car to select my outfit from amongst the others I had. I grabbed a white lab coat, stethoscope, clip board and clipped the I.D card that I had stolen from the hospital to the label of the lab coat. I had already altered I.D replacing the photo with a photo of myself. I was ready I put my keys in my pocket and headed to work my persona for this day Dr. J. Eddie.

I walked inside the hospital through a side entrance. It was still early in the morning. I picked up a stack of paperwork, clipped it to the clipboard and began my hustle. I blended into my environment like the clouds in the sky. I proceeded up the stairs onto the next floor. Ahead of me enclosed in a conference office sitting at a large, long oval table were doctors, nurses, and staff members having their early morning meeting.

I continued my journey down the corridor and located the assignment board. I viewed the schedule as to what doctors were scheduled to do what and at what time. I wrote that information down along with their names on the clipboard I was carrying. It was time to locate their offices.

I made my way through the emergency ward and picked up some papers that was lying around and then got onto the elevator, pushing the button to the floor that led to the doctor's offices I had chosen in accordance with the schedule. Once I located the doctor's offices I went inside. If I happened to encounter a front desk receptionist, I would greet them with a good morning in my educated voice.

"Good morning," she would reply. "Can I help you?"

"Yes," I'd reply, "is the Dr. in his office?" Me knowing that he wasn't.

"Not right now," she says, "the Dr. is scheduled to do surgery at this moment."

"Well, I have some important paperwork for him, is it alright if I leave it in his office?"

"Sure, go ahead," she said.

"Thank you." I replied!

Once in the doctor's office I quickly began looking for the doctor's pants or jacket. It only took a few minutes to his billfold in one or the other. I removed the billfold took the last two credit cards from behind the others, then neatly replacing the wallet back where I got it from. On the way out of the office I bid the receptionist a good day.

"Thank you," she replied.

walked down the corridor to the elevator, pushed the button and waited for the elevator to arrive. I stepped in the elevator, pushed the button to the main floor where I would continue hustling. I walked past several offices, until I come upon one that wasn't occupied. I went into the office with my ears in wolf mode tuned to any and all sounds outside the office. I looked under and, in the desk, found nothing then I looked behind the door. On the handle was a purse so I looked inside there it was a trifold lady's wallet. I swiped up two credit cards replaced the wallet neatly back inside the purse, pushed the door back and exited the office.

Now that I had four credit cards it was time to go. I left the hospital and went to where my car was parked. I pressed the automatic car starter the car came to life; I hop in nonchalant and drive off just as calm. I headed in the direction towards my favorite location the Peabody mall. I purchased an assortment of expensive items. Being that it was close to Christmas I included all types of interior Christmas house decorations. From there I made my way over to the electronic store, where I purchased a fifty-inch flat screen TV using one of the doctor's credit cards. The TV was so big back then, that when I got to the car; I had to take it out of the box in order for it to fit into the backseat of the car.

I went to several more stores where I purchased what was at that time the newest electronic item, a DVD player along with an assortment of DVD movies. At the jewelry store when the salesclerk who I assumed was in her twenties asked me what type of doctor I was? I told her that I was a pediatrician. I played on her femininity started flirting so it was not a problem when I purchased a men's diamond ring because she never asked me for any form of ID.

After making numerous trips from my car to the mall there was no space in the backseat of the car, nor the trunk the car was completely filled with bags and boxes. I left from the mall and drove to a gas station, filled my car up with always the best gas and selected a car wash. Along the way I picked up a copy of the Boston Globe.

I was famished and it was time to get something to eat I selected an Asian restaurant. I parked the car went inside to sit at the bar. When the bar tender came over, I ordered an appetizer Asian shrimp cocktail with a Cape Cod, I asked that my drink to be made with double cross vodka and Ocean Spray cranberry juice. I sat at the bar reading the Boston Globe waiting for my drink and appetizer.

It didn't take long for the bar tender to return with my drink and appetizer. Then he asked, "Sir would you like to order?"

"Yes." I spoke. "I'll have the string bean garlic chicken and General TSO's chicken".

After I paid for lunch with one of the credit cards.

# The City of Lynn

"Lynn, Lynn the city of sin, you never come out the same way you came in". Is a saying that started during prohibition in the early1920's, when Lynn was known for its bootleggers and prostitutes. I was residing in Lynn after moving from Salem, another historically rich city in Mass known for a completely different and even more famous reason I won't get into. Let's just say those witches are crazy man no pun intended. I was a hustler and so I needed to know the ways and the people of Lynn. As time went by, I had made good with several individuals who owned and operated small businesses within the city. To my benefit much like me they had larceny in their hearts, and I like them was looking for an opportunity to save and make extra money.

I was out hustling it seemed as if I wasn't going to have a successful day with the credit card hustle. It was getting close to noon, so I had to resort to another type of grift that was the take fast. As I was driving something inside of me said pull into this office supply super store. The store sold everything from computers and laptops to printers and just about everything one would need in office supply. This was a very large store. I noticed that the store had two entrances. One was in the front, the main entrance where they sold the store items. Then at the left side entrance, customers could mail out letters or boxes, and make copies.

However, the way the opening was on the side, you could use the left entrance to slip into the store without anyone being the wiser. I entered through that way, they never knew I was there most times. The place was busy with customers on both sides of the store. I quickly made my way from the left into the main part of the store, making sure that I stayed to the furthest side of the store which kind of hid me from view.

I finally made it to the furthest end of the store. I looked around to see if any workers were around, when I saw no workers around in the area, I walked through the swinging doors marked employees which took me into the loading warehouse area. The shelves were stocked with all kinds of office supplies, new laptops, computers, everything was right there pallets loaded with of all sorts of items!

I walked around trying to figure out how I was going to get some of those items from out of the warehouse, and out of the store without getting caught. I noticed steps that led down my Wolf ears went up. I went down the stairs it led to a lower basement area with very little lighting, just enough for me to see in the shadows. The basement area was very large. I'd say it was the complete area of the store itself. I continued walking around out of hustler's curiosity.

There were plenty of empty boxes, unassembled office chairs, and other items. Being that the area wasn't lite up very well at the further end I could see an exit sign lit up in red! I walked over there was a metal door that had a push handle alarm. I had encountered these types of emergency doors before. I knew that all I had to do was push the clamp on the side of the door and the door will open without setting off the alarm. It worked the door opened without setting off the alarm. I placed something I had found in the basement between the door to keep it from closing and locking.

There was a little lighting and some more stairs that went up through the door where to I no idea had, but I was going to find out. I was able to go up the stairs with no problem even though there was very little light. I came upon another door. I didn't notice any kind of alarm attached so I pushed on the door until it opened up. To my surprise I was looking outside the parking lot where I had parked was five, maybe six yards away!

I closed the door and retraced my steps. I went up to the warehouse, took two computer tower boxes downstairs. Then went back up for two more and brought them down in the basement also. I took the four boxes two at a time to the back subbasement door and up the stairs out the second door. I opened the door there was a red shopping cart right there on the sidewalk within arm's reach. I retrieved it put the four boxes of computers into the shopping cart, and casually rolled the cart to where I was parked hitting the automatic start. I put everything in the car, got in the car, drove out the parking lot nonchalant. Computers were a luxury item during that time.

I took those computers to one of the many business owners in Lynn that I had been doing business with. He owned a car accessory detail shop and he paid me six hundred dollars for all four computers. He was one of my main go to guys. The word began getting around in Lynn amongst a certain group of people that I was getting and selling quality items. So, I was getting requests for a number of items such as computers, printers, phone fax machines, and laptops. I had no problem filling their requests I was getting paid quite well.

I would be doing a lot of business for those business owners as time went by, I became more acquainted with business owners of "Sin of Sity". One day I decided to take a chance and let one of the owners in on one of my grifts. I asked this owner if he would be interested in doing a credit card hustle. The hustle was he would ring up curtain items in his store, but he wouldn't actually be giving me those items. I would then get 50% from each transaction. However, I made a deal with him that I wanted to accumulate enough credit so that I could get what I really wanted. That was to have him detail my Lincoln with the newest state of the art automatic starting alarm system, tint the windows, and get an expensive pull-out CD player stereo, separate DVD player (they didn't come all in one back then) with screens for the headrest, and extra car speakers, plus installation. The owner said let's do it, and if you thought the white Lincoln was bad before. Now I was really rolling like I was muthafuckan president.

# Hustling In Boston

Roxbury, Mass serves as the "heart of Black culture in Boston." Roxbury was one of the first towns in the Massachusetts Bay Colony in the 1600's and became a city in the mid 1800's until annexed or assigned back to Boston later on that same century. For those that live there well we like to call it the "Hood". The sounds of the city mixed in with the early morning energy awakened me. It was time for me to get to work. I rose up from the bed sat on the edge and looked out the window from my third-floor apartment. The city sky was in the early morning, and it was still dark blue. In the distance the orange light of the sun was climbing up over the eastern horizon bringing its welcoming light to the city of Boston. As I contemplated my hustle for today, I extended both of my arms upwards, stretching out the stiffness of the night from out my neck and body.

I made my way towards the bathroom and once inside I relieved my bladder. Afterwards I turned on the shower, adjusted the temperature, undressed and stepped inside the lukewarm water awakened me. Five minutes later I was toweling off. I wrapped the towel around my waist returned to the bedroom to prepare myself for my job "HUSTLER."

Today's attire was dress slacks, shirt and tie, with a pair of well-polished Florsheim shoes. I checked my appearance in the mirror. I was ready for whatever situation I may need to step into. Be it a businessman, manager, or even a teacher I would be dressed for the part. I stepped outside into the cool air and slipped into hustle mode.

As I walked to Dudley station, in the distance I heard the sound of the orange line turning just a few minutes away from the station. I had to run if I was going to catch the train. I went up the stairs, jumped over the turnstile avoiding the fare. If I was going to get into Downtown Boston early, I did not have time to stop and pay. I made my way into the train amongst the masses of passengers on their way to their destinations. "Ding ding", the doors closed all that was heard was the rumbling sound of the train wheels against the rail.

I sat down and waited as the train made its way down the track heading into downtown Boston. Passengers got off and on at their perspective stops. Down into the tunnel a couple stops later the sound of the bell rang again "Ding-ding", the conductor's voice announced "State Street" over the intercom. This was my destination. Making my way through the tide of people I stepped out off the train on to the platform. I made my way through the bowels, and funky smells of piss mixed with the late night before. Together with the people of Boston I went up the stairs into the clear morning air of downtown Boston.

The city pedestrians were everywhere moving in different directions making their way towards their destinations. As for me there was no certain direction. I had dealt with this situation many times before. I knew that my hustler's instinct would guide me, so I kept walking around Boston. It was still early in the morning, just the way I liked things. Knowing that most of the stores were not open for business yet, I had learned through countless encounters, that many of their doors were still opened for staff to enter.

I continued on my journey waiting for that moment to hit me, and then it did. Across from where I was, I noticed that people were going into a side door of what was either Jordon Marsh, or Filenes. It seemed like a few minutes after the people went in, the same people would exit holding in their hands what seemed like a cup of coffee with a small bag for a muffin or bagel. I crossed over to that side of the street to investigate.

I peered from outside into the window of the store. It was a small coffee and pastry shop. There were no customers in there yet, I didn't see any workers at the counters either. This was my opportunity! Quickly without hesitation I opened the door, went inside looking to my right I noticed that there was a rope that separated the main store from the coffee shop. A sign was attached to the rope that read, "Store opens at 9 do not enter."

I didn't give it much thought. I just continued to the back of the shop. I didn't see anyone back there. So, I started looking around for anything worth value. I didn't find anything of value just pots, pans, and floor utensils. I heard some voices in conversation my wolf ears went up I did not know where these people were, so I had to be more watchful. I continued looking and saw nothing.

I was about to leave when I noticed a metal door on the back end of the wall. I don't know why but my curiosity stuck me. I walked over to the area and opened up the metal door. When I looked inside, I noticed a metal ladder attached to the back part of the wall. This ladder went up the wall as far as I could see. There was more than enough space for me to climb inside, so I did.

I began climbing up the metal ladder, about five feet up I came upon another metal door. I opened it exited out into what must have been the back stock area of the department store. I headed back inside continuing to climb further up the ladder. Each floor there was a metal door, every time the results were the same, another department's back stockroom. I climbed down to what was the luggage department, grab up a large canvas bag and returned back into the ladder. I climbed up and exited out into the men's stockroom department. I selected high end items like Armani, and Ralph Lauren designer suits, Calvin Klein jeans, Lacoste, Gucci, and Polo T shirts. I folded each and every item so I could fit as much as I could in that canvas bag. I was ready to go!

I heard customers on the floor shopping. I peeked out from my location saw that the store was now open to the public. It must have been hustler's luck. Anyway, I came out from the stockroom to my advantage the men's bathroom was to the opposite side. With my hustle sack draped over my shoulder I quickly left the stock area went over into the men's bathroom and waited. When no security personal came into the bathroom, I knew that it had to be okay.

I left the bathroom went out on the main floor. I mingled in with the other shoppers. I could see that I was being followed by security "floor walkers" waiting for me to take something and out it in the bag. I walked around acting as if I was going to actually take something but did not. I made my way to the exit and walked out of the store while the Floor walkers thought I came in with the bag the whole time. Just several blocks away from where I was at is the combat zone. I had been through the combat zone on several occasions it was a rough and tough part of Boston, so I knew what type of people operated within the "ZONE".

The combat zone was the red-light district with strip clubs, bars, hoes, hookers, pimps, and drugs, just about every negative aspect of the dark side. I don't know if it was truth or rumors, but it was said by everyone in Boston that the zone was run by the Italian mob at that time.

# BIG TONY

Who else but my guy Tony. I went to The Intermission club on Washington Street. It appeared to be opened, with my hustle sack in tow, I crossed the street. I pulled at the front door and entered. I was confronted same always by the 200-pound Gorilla looking Italian guy dressed in black. He knew who I was, he knew the business, and why I was there. He asked me to wait at the front door entrance until he returned.

As I waited, I took in the show of half-dressed females walking around. Mr. Muscle returned then pointed me in the direction of one of the many booths. I walked over to the booth, sitting there was Tony. He dressed casually in a Polo shirt with some of buttons unbuttoned, to showcase several large gold chains around his neck. On his wrist was a masculine gold watch, on his other wrist was a handsome sized gold I D bracelet. He wore several diamond clustered rings on his fingers. This guy was all business and definitely in charge.

"So, my friend, what do you have today?" he asked.

"Some quality men's suits and men's clothing," I said. "Let me show you what I have." I removed several clothing items and passed them over for him to take a look at. He viewed the suits as well as the other items with interest.

"Listen," he said. "I might have a few associates that I thinks would also be interested in what you're selling if you have a few minutes."

"Sure," I said.

"Wait right here," he said.

As he stood up and went to his office. I sat back enjoying the scenery of half-naked strippers walking round shaking ass as I waited for Tony to return. Ten minutes later three guys walked into the club and went straight to the office. Few more minute go by, Tony comes out of the office over to where I was sitting with the three guys that came in earlier,

"Let's see what you have," said an unknown voice from the group,

"You have some quality suits," came a reply.

"How much are you asking for the suits?"

"I want to sell everything as a bundle," I said. Other than the one suit that I am keeping for myself, I made a deal for everything at a reasonable price that made all involved more than happy. Before I left the club Tony asked if I wanted to hang around for a while.

"Sure," I said, and he said with a smile,

"Get anything you want, whatever you want to do!"

I hit that store for good least six months snatching all kinds of crazy high-end merchandise until the day I got caught. It resulted in me getting arrested, and a trip to Deer Island.

However, that wasn't my only hustle in the city in the same location. There was another high-end store called Jordan Marsh. I came upon this one during another hustle. I noticed it out the corner of my eye, and then came back later like I always do. I was up very early in the morning and downtown before most businesses opened. On one of those days, I decided to check the entrance of the delivery dock. I went up the stairs to look and there were no workers on the dock. I made my way through the delivering area into the main store.

The store was not open to the public at that time so there were very few lights on, casting a dark silhouette I went into wolf mode. I did hear maintenance workers, but I was now dressed in what was considered serious business attire so if I ran into any of the workers, I'd play it like I might own this muthafucker. I began making my way around the store having a selection of just about anything I wanted in the store.

I noticed that every item that I wanted had an alarm attached to them that would be no problem at all. I knew where the alarm remover was located behind any one of the cashier counters. With tool in hand, I removed alarms from all clothing items. I always made sure to put the alarm remover back behind the counter. I went to the Intermission club in the zone Tony always made sure I left with money in my pockets and good time.

# MONEY, MONEY and MONEY

It was an unusually cold winter morning in Boston. I made a decision to wear two layers of clothing to maintain the warmth in my body. I wore jogging pants under my dress pants and a wife beater under my shirt. I stepped out of my apartment that day as early as possible into the cold air, making sure that I would be able to catch the earliest orange line train into Boston. The train pulled into the downtown stop at State Street that's where I exited the subway. This was my stop. making my way up the stairs from the bowels of the train station and into street of downtown Boston. I only had to walk a couple of blocks to reach my usual hustle destinations Filenes or Jordon March. I went to the loading dock and entered the store from there and into the main store.

It was very early in the morning so most of the lights in the store were not turned on. In the echo of the store, I heard the early morning sounds of voices and machines that were being used by the maintenance crew workers. Even the escalators were turned off at that time, so I was going up them step by step until I reached the floor of the men's department.

I went straight to the expensive suits and began grouping curtain suits on the rack that I was going to take with me. It took me a good fifteen to twenty minutes, and then I shot over to the shirt department to get shirt items. That's when my wolf ears went up. In the close distance I heard two female employees in a discussion as one employee was training the other. I could feel my hustler's intuition kick in like a Jedi feeling the force. I don't know why but I walked over to investigate, that was when I came upon a surprise. I couldn't believe what I was seeing. There in plain view on top, behind the counter had to be twenty plus black register trays and each one held lots of money!

I went behind the counter and started taking loot out of the trays all the while keeping my ears tuned into the conversation that was coming from the back so as to know where they were. I took the largest bills first: $100s, $50s and then $20 dollar bills. I was folding bills together putting the cash in every possible pocket that I had, then I began taking the $10- and $5-dollar bills.

I was satisfied with what I had gotten so it was time for me to get out of there. However, I had not realized how much time had gone by. I went to the delivery dock hoping to exit the way I had entered, but there were six to seven workers unloading several trucks it was looking too risky.

Yes, I thought to myself the employee's entrance exit. When I got to the employee's entrance standing on duty was an unarmed twenty something young African American female security guard that weighed no more than ninety-five pounds. I wasn't going to let this young lightweight female stop me from leaving the store with a score like this. I walked straight for the door, she stepped in front of me and asked, "May I see your employee's identification please."

I paid her and her request no attention; I walked straight through her pushing right past her and out the store into the street. She was right behind me but did not make an attempt to stop me physically. I heard her words, "Excuse me sir, sir!" She repeated herself again and again. I also heard the sound of static from her walkie talkie I just kept walking. I never changed pace blending into the waves of pedestrians that covered the sidewalks of the city, making sure to zag around corners, up and down streets getting further away increasing my distance.

When I heard the sounds of multiple police sirens cutting through the morning air, I knew that they had to be looking for me. That's when I remembered I had on a double set of clothing. I ducked inside a building, located the bathroom, once inside I riffled through the garbage can and grabbed an empty bag and went inside an empty stall. I took off my pants, shirt leaving me in a jogging suit. I removed all the money from my pockets and put it into the empty bag. On my way out of the bathroom I discarded the extra clothing in the bathroom waste basket. I exited out of the building; I began walking still not too fast, but at a pace with speed. I knew I had to get out of the city. I switched my walk up, I began walking down the street as if I had a leg problem faking a limp as I made my way to the closest subway station.

I saw a lady who seemed was heading in the same direction that I was.

"Excuse me, ma'am," I said in what was my best country accent.

"Can you help me please"? "I'm trying to get to North station", "but I believe that I must have gotten off at the wrong stop".

"Someone told me that there's a train station somewhere around here that I should catch in order to get to where I need to be"

"Sure," she said. "

"As a matter of fact, I'm headed to that station, and you can tag along with me I'll show you".

The unsuspecting lady didn't realize that she was the cover I needed in order to get away out of the city. As she and I walked together towards the train station I noticed a policeman on foot patrol. I watched him from the corner of my eyes he was looking at me and was on his police radio. I played it cool walking with my fake limp in accompanying by my unsuspected female companion. The two of us indulged in conversation making it seem as if the two of us were friends on our way to the train station. When she and I got to the station she explained to me what I needed to do to get where I was going. I thanked her and I waited somewhat nervously for the train to arrive. Once on the train I was more at ease. It was a close call, but the WOLF had slipped away into the substation.

I had the money, but I also had a serious cocaine habit. Once I had made it back to the hood I knew where to go to get what I wanted. I purchased two hundred dollars' worth of nose candy from then went to my usual location to get high. I knocked on the door and a female friend of mine opened up. She was no stranger we hugged and kissed.

"So baby, what's going on with you?" I asked her.

"Nothing much," she replied.

She knew what I was there to do. We exchanged small talk as she went to go get what paraphernalia was needed to get high.

"You want something to drink?" she asked me.

"Sure, what do you have?"

"Beer," she said.

"That'll work."

She sat down next to me on the couch handed me a beer with a glass trey and gold straw. I was always comfortable at her place. We hit about 50s worth of the blow and did our thang. I left her apartment high and satisfied. That habit of mine was causing my game to slip the money that I was getting was more for the blow then what it should have been.

My ability to make intellectual decisions was all wrong. I was rushing my process and making bad decisions. Sniffing cocaine had proven to be counterproductive to my goals, as well as what I represented. I struggled with that habit until I finally got control of it and stopped getting loaded but it took its toll.

After years of going in and out of prison I eventually got myself back in a hustler's state of mind. I was back in the game and productive. I stepped up my hustle got more into the credit card game spending time in any number of Boston notable downtown lounges, restaurants and bars. Always ordering Johnny Walker Scotch whiskey in the blue label, or XO cognac nothing but top shelves liquors. I would always be studying, reading the Boston Globe, Lawyer's Weekly, or the Wall Street Journal. Going to those high-end locations enabled me to socialize rub elbows with people of importance such as lawyers, executives, and important businesspeople. I'd immerse myself into the conversation with the suits with the intent of gathering knowledge and information.

I believed that in doing so I was not only making my face a familiarity within the business world. I believed that if I would happen to encounter any one of those individuals in their place of business, not only would I have the ability to communicate with them on their level. I would also be somewhere in their sub-conscience. They would somehow recollect that they knew me from somewhere, somehow, and that I did have a reason for being in whatever place of business I was in.

I was a master mind at finding my way into all sorts of buildings, high quality restaurants, exclusive clubs, sometimes even in secluded closed locations. I took advantage of the commodities that were available in most of those places. Swiping top shelf liquors, quality champagnes, Kolby stakes, lobsters, you name it. Many occasions I got my hands on bank cash bags or money from out of safes that were left unlocked and un-attended.

I was enjoying and reaping the benefit of the lifestyle of the rich. Everything that I had purchased was with boosted credit cards from; clothing, to jewelry, gas for my car, car washes, groceries, even nights out on the town, or when I would travel. I just about had anything that I wanted we ever I wanted it.

I was getting in and out of all sorts of building throughout the Boston area. There was this one building that in the lower basement was what is known as a phone bank. It's a place where people used phones to raise money called a telethon. I had this idea I recorded some elevator music on this handheld recorder that I had at home. The next step, well here it goes.

The first thing first was to get some credit cards. I went into the downtown crossing area to a place where I knew I would be successful in accomplishing that task. The Ivy league college up the street. I knew a side back way into the college that allowed me to bypass the security guard at the front entrance desk. Once inside of the college I walked down the hallway and picked up several books so I would blend in with all the other students. I would do this during a time when all if not most of the professors were busy in class teaching, giving me a wide selection of offices to go into and do my thing. It took me no time to gaffel up several cards mission accomplished.

I exited the college the same way that I went in unnoticed. I went to the building, slipped pass security there, took an elevator to the basement where the phone bank was located. Time for the wiggle I went to doing what I had planned. I dialed Eastern Union Gram.

"Hello Eastern Union," a women's voice said on the other end, "may I help you?"

"Good morning." I spoke. "Yes" an associate of mine had his wallet stolen last night and he has no money or I.D. he needs to return back home. I was wondering if it's possible for me to wire him some cash."

"Yes, you can," she said, "and how much would you like to send him?"

"$500", I said.

"How would you be paying sir" she asked.

"I'll be using a credit card." I said then I gave her all the necessary information of the card. "In conclusion" I said, "He doesn't have any form of I.D. so we're going to use a password. "Rumpelstiltskin" was the password.

She said that she needed a callback number, so I gave her the number that was on the phone I was using. I hung up the receiver and waited. A few minutes passed and the phone rang. I answered it disguising my voice to sound more like a female.

"Good morning" I referred to the name on the credit card, Smith and Taylor. "May I help you?"

"Yes," said the lady on the opposite end, "Can I speak to Mr. Smith?"

"Yes," I said. "Can you hold for a minute." I activated the tape playing the music I had recorded. I waited as the music played. Then I turned off the music and answered, "Mr. Smith may I help you?"

"Yes, this is Eastern Union gram, did you authorize a $500 wire payment to a Mr. James Johnson?"

"Yes, I did." I said, "and the password is Rumpelstiltskin."

"Alright," she said and that was that.

I gathered up my things, left the building and headed to the nearest Eastern Union gram office. Everything went as I hoped it would and I was $500 richer in the game! I did that at least twice a month. I never got caught for that hustle but using stolen credit cards would catch up with me eventually, it took several years before law enforcement realized it was me that they were looking for.

I attempted to be as careful as possible every time I went shopping. I would hold my head down when entering any store, and always looked downward when I paid for items at the cash register upon leaving the store, since more and more cameras started to get installed in places over the years. This day I recalled it was in the evening and I was shacked up the house with my lady watching TV. She was in the kitchen cooking dinner. I heard something outside and looked out the living room window. I noticed a white guy outside with a camera taking pictures. I went outside and confronted him.

"What are you doing out here taking pictures?" I asked him. He explained to me that he was a realtor and was taking pictures of the neighborhood. Someone was interested in buying the house that was empty on the right side of ours. It seemed feasible to me, so I didn't think anything more of it. The next warning happened a few days later day in the evening. I returned home with my lady from a night on the town and noticed that one of our outside garbage cans was missing. I had thought that one of the teenage juveniles in the hood had stolen it.

It wasn't until I went to court with the information from my paid lawyer that I learned not only was I being watched, but detectives were taking photos, and it was them who had taken that garbage can! They were hoping to find receipts that I used to purchase items with stolen credit cards. When that moment finally arrived, they came deep there was no less than fifteen police officers, and no less than five detectives. They wanted to be certain that I didn't slip out the back door. What they didn't know was that I too had been planning for that moment. I made a secret hiding place, I watched as they looked all over the house for me. I even heard someone say, "come out we know that you're here." I waited and waited but they weren't leaving so I came out of my hiding place to their surprise!

# The life of this HUSTLER

I was always true to the game of hustling, so as the saying goes the hustle game was true to me. After living and hustling in Boston for many years I was a professional at what I was doing, it for surely showed. I wore the finest suits. I enjoyed the best meals, at some of the most exclusive restaurants around. I walked in Bostonians and Italian shoes. I wore diamond rings of different cuts, precious stones, gold bracelets, necklaces, Gucci down to my socks. Weather I was at home or on the road life was a breeze. I did some extensive traveling throughout these United States I ran through New York, California, Florida, Washington D.C., Las Vegas and other states always in first class accommodations.

I treated all my females like queens even the ones that I didn't love. I enjoyed playing the role of a man of means going to upscale entertainment events and lounges at night. When I would entertain myself in the company of a beautiful lady, we would go to one of Boston's high class hotel restaurants.

I would sit at the bar or in the lounges dressed up like a tycoon Wall Street paper in hand, order a smooth pour of Hennessy Paradis Cognac and play the muthafuckan role. If I wanted to be really debonair, I indulge on the limited pleasure of the crown jewel Louis XIII sipping it slowly as I read the Robb Roberts Report.

In this kind of lifestyle, you get to meet certain people that can provide certain things. One of those things back then was being able to purchase Cuban cigars. Paired with the Cognacs the two together are an exceptional match. I paid for that lifestyle at someone else's expense. My dress code was that of a boss, I knew the rudiments of time and its appropriation when it came to style and swagger. My look said money, but my money spoke volumes for me. I always maintained an executive appearance haircut trimmed nice and tight, compliments of my personal barber Binky over at Stars Barber.

# PAUL PIERCE NEW YEARS

The year is 2003 a momentous event was occurring in Boston. # 34 Paul Pierce of the Boston Celtics was having a New Year's Eve party, an extravaganza event that included a fashion show highlighting some of Boston's finest and sexiest female models. It was hosted by Boston radio station 1090 WILD. This information I received from my lady, who in turn got it from her sister. The plan was for me and wifey to meet her sister and boyfriend in the lobby of the hotel where the event was being held. I was at the summit of my hustling game ready for any peek of opportunity, so attending this event at the asking price of one thousand dollars a ticket was no problem. I purchased two VIP tickets, however when the time came my lady's sister and her male friend backed out. I knew that in reality they were perpetrating a fraud, especially with the lame ass excuse they gave.

It was winter and cold outside the day of the event. I took the day off from hustling and spent it with my girl preparing for the upcoming event. It was about six o'clock in the evening I made a call to a friend. He and I had spoken previously. He said that he would pick my lady and I up from the house drive us to the hotel were the event was taking place.

He was on his way. My cell phone started ringing and I answered it. My friend was outside waiting for us in his silver BMW. You know we had to come in style chauffer and the whole 9 yards. I always liked to pour the character on smooth. We arrived at the Hyatt Regency in Cambridge Massachusetts around seven o'clock. I thanked my friend for the ride my girl and I went into the hotel to the front desk to check in we had reservations for a room as well, picked up our keys and went to our room.

The event was scheduled to begin at eight o'clock. We took a shower together, got dressed for the occasion headed out, closing the door behind us we rode the elevator down to the lobby. We walked into the event stupendously clean. I was dressed in a three-piece black suit from Filene's with a white tux shirt, and black bow tie. My lady companion was super sexy in her simulated diamond studded black elegant gown, with matching shoes from Lords and Taylor, a tennis diamond bracelet, several diamonds rings, and a gold watch with a black watch band to compliment everything. Everything we wore I purchased with cards that I had gotten so you know we were both stunting looking like a million plus.

I presented our names we were given tickets then escorted to the VIP section. where a card was on top of the table with my last name printed on it. I pulled out the chair for my lady to sit down and I joined her sitting in the chair next to her. In attendance were all types of famous people, legendary sport players like Red Sox slugger David "Big Poppy" Ortiz, Manny Ramirez, and all-time great pitcher Pedro Martinez, as well as other Boston sport superstars and notables.

The music was jamming over the music the local D J welcomed us all to this momentous occasion. I spent some time with my lady, and then excused myself from the table to circulate. I was walking around taking in the atmosphere seeing who was there. While strolling around my hustle's intuition got to tingling, I noticed that at one of the many bars there was a long line of VIP guests waiting for a drink. I went over to the bar some of the people waiting in line where there to buy a bottle of Champagne and some other single drinks. The reason for the long line was that there only appeared to be one person attending to the patrons.

I went into hustle mode as quick as a snap. My mind started thinking, I noticed the similarity in the way I was dressed in comparison to the outfit the bartender was dressed in, we both had tuxes on with a bowtie. I then noticed the people paid for their drinks and Champagne with cash. This must have been a cash only bar. I casually walked behind the bar like I owned it, stationed myself at the opposite end of the bar, gave the other bartender a nod then began asking patrons can I help you! I was selling bottles of Salon champagne each at $300 a bottle.

Each sale I pretended I was putting the money in the cash drawer, but I was actually putting the majority of the cash in my pocket and the rest in the tip bucket, which also went to me. After selling about six bottles I excused myself and went back to where I was sitting to give my lady friend the money that I had pocketed. I waited a few minutes to see if anyone was going to say something me. No one did so I returned back to the bar and continued hustling. That sleight of hand hustler moment grossed me no less than $4000 along with two bottles of that fine Salon Champagne. My lady and I partied like super stars all through the late night into the New Year's all at the expense of the patrons and Paul Peirce the whole night ended up paying for itself.

# NEW YEARS DAY

Other than the sound of the air conditioner, the hotel room was quiet. The curtain to the windows were pushed to both sides of the window frame revealing the Boston city lights. I got up out of the bed walked over to the window to admire the scenery of the lights twinkling reflecting off the Charles River. Towards the right in the distant was the silhouette of the city of Boston while darkness loomed in the backdrop.

I returned to the bed lying up against the cool side of the pillow, caught up in the moment reflecting back on all past events. I moved over close to my lady, wrapped my arm around her and dozed off to sleep. I awakened as always early the next morning unable to return back to sleep by something that was a part of me, the early morning hunger of the hustle. I got up from the bed, went to the bathroom took a quick shower and got dressed. Before heading out the room I kissed my lady on the forehead.

She turned softly in the comfort of the Egyptian cotton sheets as I headed out the room to explore the surroundings around the hotel. I followed my hustling instincts as I made my way down the hotel hallways. I didn't encounter anyone along the way. It was way too early. I began checking door after door they were locked. I headed downstairs to the hotel lobby. I heard people talking, which emanated from somewhere behind the front counter. There was a door that I could tell from its location was the back entrance to the front counter.

I turned the handle the door was unlocked. I opened the door slowly then peeked in. It was the back area behind the front desk. Off to my right was a large safe I could see that the door was slightly ajar. My wolf ears went up. The conversation that I was hearing was coming from two workers stationed at the front lobby counter their backs were towards me. I made my assessment of the situation calculated my move with precision.

I stepped into the back area, moving as quickly as possible, make as little noise as possible it was like walking on rice paper. As I went towards the safe, I grabbed a fist full of bills off the safe's shelf, then just as swiftly retreated backwards into the hallway lobby with the quick fast. I continued hustling as my hustler instinct continued calling from within.

I noticed to the left of the corridor was an opening with steps that went down to a lower level. I headed down the stairs which lead to a gate that was slightly opened. I continued walking in constant awareness to ever possible sound around me like a wolf stocking its prey. I heard the sound of someone moving bottles clanging coming from a back room to my left on one of the chairs was a suit jacket.

I removed the jacket from the back of the chair checked the inside pocket for a billfold. There was one! I looked through the billfold there was some cash about eighty dollars, but that's not what I wanted. I took the back two credit cards placed the billfold back in the inner pocket of the jacket like the wind I was gone. I headed up the stairs, caught the elevator back upstairs to my hotel room to order some mimosa for breakfast room service sound good.

# Out into the city

"Wake up baby." I said I as I shook her delicately.

"It's almost lunch time, are you hungry?"

She had no idea what had transpired. She got out of bed, I kissed her, and she went to the bathroom to shower. I turned on the television and when she returned my attention was drawn to her naked body. I watched her as she dolled up rubbing herself all over her body with scented lotion, a little body powder then she applied perfume all over her sexy body. she got dressed and we headed out. Closing the door behind us the first stop was the lobby.

"Good afternoon," I said to the front desk clerk. "I would like to extend our stay for two more days and nights, how much will that be?" I paid then we went for lunch. I was dressed in my full-length trench coat with a blue suit and tie, my lady was dressed in concordance. It was cold she wrapped her arm in mine we headed to the Cambridge side galleria mall. Kay's Jeweler I knew what to do.

I went into role play with my lady close to me. I directed her towards the saleslady. She greeted us,

"Good evening may I help you?"

"Yes," I said. "Today we're celebrating ten years together I want to get my lovely wife something special, what do you recommend?"

The sales lady smiled with appreciation showed us a couple items then she informed me that due to the holidays most items in the store were marked 50% off. One of my rules was to never be in a hurry to buy anything so I played it off. I was the loving husband with a pleasant demeanor. I saw what I wanted. It was a diamond sapphire bracelet with a matching ring.

"How much is the dual set?" I asked the sales representative, "Good choice, sir." She spoke.

My game was in full effect. My lady tried the items on she gleamed with admiration. "I think this is it." I said as I handed the saleslady one of the three credit cards I had in my possession. She gave no indication of suspicion she didn't ask me for an ID. With one swipe of the card the sale was quickly approved so I knew I had a reliable card.

She handed the bag to my lady along with a New Year salutation and I returned the salutation. It was time to keep working these credit cards, so we went shopping throughout the mall, with every use I rotated each card.  I knew that by doing that it allowed the first card to rest as I used the other ones before using the first card again. On the way out of the mall just for the hell of it I bought myself a remote control black four door BMW car. As we made our journey back to the Hyatt, we did it as if we were tourists out doing some sightseeing along the way.

We were getting cold it was time to get out of the New England winter weather. We went up to the room to put all the items we had purchased in our hotel room. I knew that some time had passed by since I had used either card, so it was time to eat. There was a restaurant located within the hotel lobby, so we headed there. I ordered two pastrami sandwiches on rye along, with a couple of Blue Hawaii's full of top shelve liquor. Those were the most delicious pastrami sandwiches I had ever tasted. I pulled a brazenly bold move, I paid the bill with one of the credit cards that I grab from downstairs early, but I knew that no one name is unique.

Back in our hotel room my lady took a shower while I watched TV. When she came out of the bathroom, I went in to shower myself when I came out of the bathroom, she was lying on the top of the bed dressed in a sexy teddy. I could see in her eyes what story had been playing in her mind. I joined her in the bed in close proximity to her soft lovely body.

The passion of her kiss engulfed my senses I locked in the pleasure of a warm French kiss. My lips explored her body. I tasted the sweetness of her warm nipples as my hands continued exploring further down until I found the soft pedal in between her flower. I rubbed it delicately until the nectar of her honey ran down my finger. Her passionate demeanor aroused my manhood I could no longer contain my own lust.   I gave into desire. We locked together in the dance of passion love making until we exploded. I wrapped her in the warmth of my arms as she drifted off into an after-love nap. The sound of the TV was all that I heard as I laid there deep into the thoughts of the past day's events.

So as not to disturb her I slowly got out of the bed, and I put my underwear back on. Making my way over to the hotel window I looked out in the evening darkness of the sky, absorbing the energy from the moon as the stars shined down on the Charles River, I smiled wolfishly within myself. I was content with my accomplishments.

My lady called to me in a sensuous way asking me to return back to the bed with her I went out like a light. The morning sun of the next day shined through the window, but winter made its presence outside. After getting dressed we headed back to the Cambridge Galleria Mall. Would the credit cards still work? In order to know I had to buy something. We went to a different jewelry store within the mall using a different tactic from the one I had used from the day before. I purchased myself a man's 18kt. gold diamond cluster ring, the 60% off reduced the price considerably making the purchase less expensive but more acceptable with the use of the credit card. The purchase was approved I was elated. We continued shopping for more items until I got the miss meal cramps it was dinner time, so I choose Italian. We went to Davio's one of the most expensive spots in the North Shore.

Our Holiday vacation was over Nina had to get back to her job, and I needed to get back to the hustling and deceiving, which were the rudiments of my job. Getting paid quick fast was always the purpose. I couldn't see myself living any other way. I had been hustling for thirty years this was the only life I had come to know.

# The Beginning

My earlier years were the teaching and learning period. It all started when I began hustling downtown St. Petersburg, Florida. I had been stealing since I was five years young, but when I was put out of the house, I had to make a living, the one thing that I was the best at was thieving. So, it became more than that as the years went by. I was up and out the door early in the mornings. I felt the warmth of the Florida sun as I made my way towards downtown. St. Petersburg downtown was the only location that was close enough and had a wide selection of department jewelry stores, coin pawn shops and antique shops.

At the beginning it was department stores. I was making chicken change but not the type of money I was making when I started hustling and stealing from the jewelry stores, coin and pawn shops. By doing this I was also getting an education. Knowledge in diamonds classifications like the four Cs of precious stones, gold other precious alloys, as well as old and new coins.

There were two particular coin shops that I had been going to on a daily basis. I was having conversation with both shop owners every time I went there, but not only was I getting in good with them.

I was also casing out and understanding the layout of each shop as well as getting information. With each visit it became clearer and clearer to me that both shops were an easy opportunity for me to snatch items all without getting noticed. In one of the shops the layout was like this. There were four large display cases on both sides of the shop as well as one large counter in the front of the store. On the right-side front of the shop behind one of the counters was a large board attached to the wall, pinned to the board was plastic money holders with a wide verity of past dated paper money inside of them.

I also noticed that most of the display cases had no locks, thus making it easy for me to get access. On this day I made casual conversation with the person working as I had been doing for a while, I made a small purchase of a coin.

After that I walked around making inquiries showing interest in other items and wasted more time looking, making keen observations. When another customer entered the store, I was left to my own devices as if I wasn't in the store. That wasn't the first time either that had happened. A few times before that day it went the same way. This day when the same events occurred, I went into wolf mode. I already knew what I wanted. In one of the display cases was a coin container with no less than ten gold Krugerrand coins. I had locked the position of its location in my mind. I looked around in every direction. The clerk was busy with the customer that had walked in a minute ago. I knew that he was the only worker.

I took my position and made one finally look as to where everyone was. It was now or never. I reached over behind the counter, opened up the display case with the position of the item already locked in my mind I took one last look, reached into the display case, grabbed the plastic coin container containing with the gold coins, closed the case and pocketed it.

I breathed a sigh of relief and relaxed. Methodically I walked out of the store out into the warmth of the Florida sunshine. I had been selling stolen items in the past to honest owners but not the owners of a coin or jewelry shop. I knew that on the market gold Krugerrands coins were somewhere in the range of $400 to $600 each. I never thought at the time I would get my hands on Krugerrands. When I walked into the shop, I knew what I had.

"What's up?" he said as I approached the counter. "I got gold Krugerrands coins." I replied. I handed five of the ten I had across the counter to him. He examined them as I knew he would then made me an offer.

"How about $300 a coin?" he said. I'm not one to bargain when the price is within reason for me; it's all about getting rid of things as soon as possible.

"Alright deal," I said. He went to the back of his shop and returned with $1,500. Handed it to me, with $1,500 in my pocket and five more coins I was done hustling for the day. Headed back to the hood, walked up 16th Street, bought some rolling paper and a four-finger lid of weed, which was at that time $40.

From there I went to the park on 16th Street smoked some weed while watching the young hood flowers go by. That's when I saw Rose.

"Say girl, what's happening?"

"Nothing," she said.

"Want to smoke?" I asked.

"Sure." she replied.

I rolled up a joint and smoked with her and talked about general things. "You want to go with me to the store?" I asked her.

"Sure," she said. We walked together laughing and talking. I purchased a bottle of Boone's Farm strawberry hill wine along with a couple of bags of BBQ chips for her and myself. "So," I asked. "Do you have anything or any place that you need to be or do?"

She said no.

"Well instead of going back to the park, do you want to go with me to my place, smoke some weed and listen to some music? I do need my hair braided."

"Okay," she said, "Let's go."

My brother Van was at the apartment when we arrived. "What's up bro? This here is Rose." She sat on the couch and rolled up a thump. I turned on the record payer, stacked some vinyl to let the music play. I went to the bathroom got the Afro shine and a couple of afro combs, came back in the room then sat on the floor between her legs.

She lit up the joint and we smoked. I passed the combs and hair grease to her. She grabbed my hair, checked its length then began braiding my hair. The music, the weed, having her grease and braid my hair was very relaxing. After she finished braiding my afro we conversed. I didn't try to make a move on her. I was happy with the time we spent together. I saw her to the door and watched as she left with her nice ass. I went back inside, took a shower and relaxed.

Besides stealing and hustling, Music was at the top of things I enjoyed. Because of my love for music, I had to have all the latest albums, but of course I wasn't going to spend money for any of the lasted albums. I was a grifter took what I wanted no one was ever the wiser. I had been going to Strawberry records snatching not only the funkiest albums, but other psychedelic items too, such as black lights, lava lamps, posters as well other far out stuff to decorate my room. The singing group Ohio Players was hot on the radio throughout the hood with songs like Skintight, Sweet Sticky thing, and Love Roller Coaster. I had been successful grabbing other albums I thought why not that album.

It was a warm afternoon the Florida sun was shining bright, and I always felt confident in my abilities. I headed outside with the conviction that I was going to listening to me some Ohio Players later on today for sure. I headed up the street towards Central Square to Strawberry's. I went inside the record store the place was busy with customers perfect I thought to myself. I walked over to the disco section checking my surrounding along the way I located the Ohio Players album and another funk joint I had been waiting jam to as well. I looked around the place was still busy, what workers I saw were helping customers no one was watching me or so I thought.

I removed the records out of their jackets turned in a way so that my back was towards the front of the store, in manner that would hide what I was doing. I lifted my shirt and put the albums slightly down my pants, then straightened out my shirt to hide what I had under my shirt and headed towards the door.

I was about to leave when two guys stopped me before I could get out the door I was busted! "Excuse me, can we get those albums tucked under your shirt"! I handed them over, from there I was escorted to the back area into an office. I was asked question while security wrote down what information I gave him. He then excused himself left the room closing the door behind him. I tried the door really quick, but it was locked. So, I waited for what seemed like hours until I heard the sound of a key going into the lock, as well and the sound of a police radio as the door was being opened.

The guy that had taken all my information from me enters accompanied by two police officers. "Stand up, turn around"! One of the officers said to me. The last sound that I heard was the sound of hand cuffs. I was put in the back of the police car and transferred to a juvenile facility to be held until I went before a white judge.

It was a sleepless night for me being that this was the first time that I was locked up. I wondered what was going to happen to me. I was awakened by the loud voices of the counselors repeating "Get up breakfast time let's go! It had to be sometime between 6 or 7. I washed my face got dressed and headed out to eat. I along with the other boys walked in line to the dining hall.

When I got there, I was glad to see a few guys that I knew from the neighborhood street. we all sat at one of the tables talking. The conversation mostly consists of what one was in for, or just basic talk about things we had done. I learned that I could be going up to the boy's school in Marianna Florida. After breakfast we all headed back to the building to clean rooms and get ready for what events they had planned for us. I went to school which was just in one room. We spent about an hour there before it was recreation time. That's when I saw that there were also teenage girls locked up in the same facility with us, but they were housed at the further end of the building.

The afternoon and evening hours were mostly for socialization time. For me that was a time to represent I did my very best to leave an impression with the girls I took my shirt off and did pushups. Once my chest and arms were pumped up, I would flex my muscles. When I'd play basketball with the fellas, I showed my basketball skills doing what I had to do to impress the girls you the wolf was always in rare form.

I wasn't an angel, but I did manage to avoid getting into any type of trouble, so when a job for cleaning the building at night came, I got it. So, when everyone one else was locked in their rooms I was out and about cleaning but enjoying the freedom of being out of my room at night. It was my first night of work the place was kind of quiet except for the mumbling of the voices of boys coming from within the rooms. My task was to sweep then mop the hallway, when I got to the furthest end of the hallway there was a double wide door which separated the boys from the girls, but at night the door was unlocked. There was a pretty young teenage girl cleaning the girl side of the unit. I had seen her before during recreation time but never spoke to her this was my opportunity.

"Say girl what's your name?" I hollered across to her.

"Linda." she replied.

"Where you from?"

"Tampa." she said.

"Oh, I've been there before. What'cha doing in here?"

"Shop lifting," she said. "Do you have any idea what's going to happen to you" I might be heading to a girl's school."

We talked for a while until I heard one of the councilor's footsteps heading our direction. "Well, I hope to see you later."

I saw her the next day during recreation period from that day on she and I spent time together. Our relationship became more than close friends. Every once in a while, when we were able, we would slip in a kiss or two sometimes, if I was quick enough, I was able to play with her tits, or get to finger fuck her. In turn she would put her hand in the inside of my pants and play with my dick.

Things were getting hot for the both of us, so we began talking and planning on having sex at night during the time that we worked. The plan was that I would meet her in her room. I watched night after night, plotting until we thought we had it down to a science. The day went by as it had always done, but tonight would be the night. I did my job like I had always done sweeping then mopping, working my way down the hallway.

Linda was standing in front of her room. I waited until the counselor began making the count. I knew the next count would be in an hour. I went into Wolf mode. I made my way to her room where she was laying in her bed. I wasted no time making my moves. I began French kissing her I was already laying on top of her. We started sexually grinding I put foot on the gas, undid her pants and begin rubbing her clit. I got a handful of pussy and cream, which made my dick harder than Chinese arithmetic. But before I could pollenate her flower, I felt a tap on my back along with the loud voice from one of the male counselors.

"What the fuck do you think you guys think you're doing?"

I wanted to say what the fuck do you think we're trying to do. The counselor grabbed me by the arm and escorted me to my room. "Let's go right now." he hollered.

Not only did I lose my job, but I didn't get my shot at that piece of ass. That was my first run in with the juvenile system, but not my last. I was sent to that facility twice and the next visit got me sent to Arthur G. Dozier School for boys.

But I did get out of boy's school the second time. I didn't go back to hustling. I got a part-time job at a malt shop. The money was alright, but I enjoyed working with and talking with the girls there, they were white. This one week when I got paid, I decided to hang out for a while in the Florida sunshine and see the movie Coffee. I finished my work for the day, picked up my check and headed home to get ready for another Friday night.

I arrived home, took a shower changed into something more in tune with Friday, then headed out downtown to cash my check. After cashing my check, I headed to the theater to see the opening of the movie 'Coffee" staring Pam Grier. I was on the opposite side of the street of the theater, so I had to cross over. As I was crossing the street, I noticed this guy that I somewhat knew, but it was the white girl that he was with that caught my attention. She was dressed in a pair of tight hot pants looking all fine and pretty.

"Yo man, what's up?" I hollered in his direction as I was crossing the street. He stopped, looked around and saw it was me. "What's up Wolf man?" he said, and we greeted one another with the seventy's style of slapping five proceeded by a what's happening man.

"Nothing," he said. "What'cha up to?" he asked me.

"I'm going to catch this movie. If you guys want to see it, I'll pay."

Before he could respond his lady friend said, "Let's do it" I purchased three tickets and we made our way to where the movie was playing to sit down. I stood up on the right side of the front aisle seat so that he could go in with his female friend.

As she's going past me to sit down, I can tell from the way she did it that she purposely turned her ass so that when she was going past me her soft but firm ass rubbed along the front of my pants, she gave me a sexy look of desire. As we waited for the movie to begin showing the three of us began talking. The inside theater lights went off and besides the light from the movie screen we were in darkness.

Pam Grier was the star of the movies that time. She was beautiful and just as fine, but the movie maker made sure to put focus on her set of big tits throughout the movie. I'm watching the movie admiring Pam's big breasts when I feel a tap on my left shoulder. It was the white chick.

I turned to see what it was that she wanted. She turns towards me and says I have a question in need of an answer. "I sure wished that I had big tits like hers. I looked at her tits and replied, "Girl you've got a nice pair tit you're damn self. Anyone including myself would find pleasure in them."

Her reply was "you think so" and then she grabbed my hand and placed it on the outside of her tank top onto one of her tits, moving my hand so as to rub her tit with my hand. I could feel that she didn't have a bra on. So, I accepted the invitation and reached under her tank top and start playing with her tit.

I felt her nipples get hard in my touch, which made my dick hard. She reaches over with her hand grabbed my erected dick began to rub it up and down like it was a toy then complimented me on how big it was. That made my ego skyrocket. I went from her tit to her hot pants unzipping the front of them partially. She wasn't wearing any panties underneath those hot pants, making what I wanted to do easier. I fingered and played with her clit until she got wet as morning dew while she moved her hips, grinding in harmony with my finger. I was so involved in finger fucking her that I forgot she was with someone.

When I looked up the guy that she was with was looking at what I was doing to his girl. Since he didn't act out, my thought was that this was going to be one of those strange situations that were going on during the 70's!

I stopped what I was doing and went back to watching the movies. As I continued watching the movie every now and then she would reach over and rub my dick. After the movie I had to get her to the house. My parents had gone on one of their spiritual retreats leaving the responsibility of the house to my older brothers, so I made a suggestion.

"If you guys have nothing planned, I have some weed and some beer at the house. If you'd like to come over, we can smoke and have a beer or two listen to some music." We all agreed and begin walking to the house she kept making sexual suggestions with her eyes towards me. As we're approaching the house you couldn't help but to hear the funky soul music coming from inside the house.

The door was unlocked when I turned the handle and welcomed them in. My brother Van was home sitting down chilling on the sofa. I could smell the after smoke of weed in the air and could tell by my brother's eyes that he was high. After introductions everyone found somewhere to sit. "Does anyone want something to drink?" I asked as I was making my way to the kitchen. She asked for a cooler everyone else wanted a beer. I returned to the living room with three cold beers and a cooler for the girl. My brother gets the party started. He pulls out a joint, passed it to me I fired it up. After taking a couple of hits I passed the joint to the girl, she takes a couple of good hits and passes the joint. The joint goes around then makes its way back to me.

I don't know if it was the weed or just that she felt comfortable, but she stood up and started dancing around the room in a very provocative manner all in harmony with the music. She sexually danced her way to where I was sitting and gave me a private dance. My brother looks in my direction then gives me the nod, I knew exactly what that meant. As the song was coming to an end, she sits down next to me looping her arm into mine. When the next song began to play, I made my move, I began whispering sweet words, sexual monotones into her ear. As I touched different parts of her body she didn't resist. My brother fires up another joint and passes it around. When it gets to me, I offered her a shotgun, turning the joint around with the lit end in my mouth I blow smoke out of the opposite end of the joint. She inhaled, placing her lips close enough so that our lips touch more like a tender kiss.

From her reaction it was time for me to take this to another level. I leaned close and whispered into her ear. "Listen girl there's no need in us playing games, not when we both know what's on our mind and what our bodies are feeling. With that understanding I know you know what I am talking about so let's make this thought a reality before this opportunity passes."

I stood up taking her hand in mine led her into the adjoining bedroom, closed the door and locked it. We began kissing there was no secret to what was going to happen. I started kissing her on the neck as my hands went on a journey of exploring different parts of her body. Under her shirt I found the joy and pleasure of her tits once again. I recapped the story into her ear about the Pam's tits in the movies, and her nipples got re-erected. I slowly lowered her onto the bed lying next to her, lifting her shirt revealing her pink erected nipples. Tenderly I started sucking them from nipple to nipple. She held me close to her breasts moaning with pleasure. As I enjoyed the sweetness of her breast with my right hand, I slowly made my way down her belly un-buttoning her hot pants all the way this time. When I rubbed the prize, it was warm with every touch of my finger her clit went from moist to wet. She responded with moans moving her hips in motion to what I was doing to her with my finger this girl had rhythm the sweet smell of pussy was in the air.

My dick was harder than a 3-day old burrito from anticipation, the look in her face said feed me. She undressed while I removed my clothing. We were butter ball naked I mounted her and directed my dick to the target, her warm wet pussy. Slowly I penetrated her she moaned with pleasure with every inch of my hard dick. It felt so good.

This was my first piece of ass. So, I went to town on that pussy in every direction possible. She's moaning, I'm sweating then I feel something wonderful stirring deep inside of me, this was it! My nut felt so good, so different as it seems to last forever, but it didn't so I went for another round. Still hard I went in again sweat running down my forehead as I continued fucking. She started breathing with excitement and she started fucking faster and faster back. Her words of passion fascinated and excited me. She kept saying fuck me baby over and over then somewhere deep inside she lets out this passionate moan saying to me that she's coming, her body jumping in small fits. I felt her pussy juice coming all over my dick then she laid back in the bed breathing with a happy look on her face. I didn't get that second nut but that was alright she got it for me. I stood up went into the bathroom and wiped the smell of sex off my genitals and body.

I put my clothing on and was about to leave the room when she asked me if it would be alright if she could lie in the bed for a while? "Sure, no problem" I say to her. I left the bedroom returned to the living room went over to my brother and he slapped me five no words needed to be said.

"Yo bro," I said. "She still in the bed butt ass naked."

I didn't have to say another word. Van knew what that meant. In a real smooth manner, he made his way to the bedroom and shut the door. I sat down on the couch, rolled a joint and smoked it. I don't know if the guy was that high, but he had his head leaned back with his eyes closed, was he asleep? I don't know. My brother exited the bedroom from the look on his face I knew he had fucked her. We're all sitting in the living room smoking weed listening to the music. A few minutes later the girl comes from out of the bedroom and sits down on the couch. I lit up another joint passed it around for everyone to smoke. Now I'm just cooling high, chilling enjoying the music. After a while the girl says that she is ready to leave the guy that she came here with gets up and the two of them leave together.

A couple of weeks later I was hanging out at the park on 16th street just chilling, smoking some weed when the guy that I ran into at the movies who was with the white girl that I had fucked was there. We talked about the other day. He said it was no problem that he understood and respected the rules of the game from that day on him and I were copasetic.

I don't recall what happened, but I was unemployed and back to doing what I do hustling to make money. I was young in the hustling game at that time, still I was making enough money that allowed me to maintain a fairly decent lifestyle. But like everything in life the more you do something the better you get. I was in it for a while already making money like a seasoned hustler.

Even thought I was a young teenager I could afford to dress more stylish than most of the young teenage guys of my age. I was always going to the dances in the latest appeal getting most of the teenage hood flower's attention and numbers. A good wolf always stayed in rare form. But I never gave any thought or consideration to what and where the way I was getting my money would take me. I learned to accept getting locked up doing time was all a part of the game. It didn't stop me from doing what had become as easy as breathing. So, every time I got caught or had to go away to do time when I got out, I went right back to what got me there. It was a vicious cycle that would shape my life for years to come.

# A.G.D. School for Boys

Arthur G. Dozier School for Boys this was just one of the many stops that I would make on my journey in the life. Dozier school for boys was huge there was a highway that separated the two compounds from each other. You would have thought that it was a summer camp school for boys there's was a12 ft. swimming pool, a recreation centers the place was a self-sustaining institution. But the place wasn't a summer camp. There was this one building known as. "The White House "If you did anything even something minor you would get the leather strap whip on your ass until it bled. Some of the boys were sexually abused by staff and older boys, some of the boys that we thought escaped you knew that most of them were killed and buried in shallow graves on boot hill. All the reason I tried to avoid certain places and areas.

The first time I was a young boy, and it was a learning lesson for me I learned that I had to be cautious but not terrified. The next time I went there I was a teenager well-schooled plus I knew several guys there who were from my hood in St. Petersburg. We all hung together forming our own little crew.

I along with other boys worked at the reformatory school meat processing plant. We slaughter and prepared cows, pigs, and chickens for not only the compound, but for the surrounding prisons and camps. If I could when I wasn't working, I would spend some of my time sharpening my boxing skills and lifting weights. I was avoiding as much trouble as possible, but this one day I had to do what was required of me based on the situation. That resulted in me getting into a fight with one of the boys from another cottage. That altercation got me sent to "The Hill."

The treatment was insane. The Hill was deep in the pine wood forest on a hill. I was placed in a lock up in a small dark damp cell for 72 hours during that 72 hour my meals three times a day were cold consistent of one boiled egg a spoon of spinach and a slice of bread no milk or juice. I had to drink the terrible tasting water from the sink in the cell.

After those 72 hours I was let out of the cell to mingle with the other boys that had made it through the same ordeal. I was weak all I could think of was the satisfying breakfast that was ahead a few days later. I was returned back into the regular population. Even though the treatment of the hill was a crime I got sent back for another infraction back to THE HIL!

I was 17 when I was released. I was healthy in excellent physical shape and thanks to watching Soul Train on Saturdays, I knew how to do just about all the latest dances. Like most guys I left there with the thought of making up for lost time. It was nine in the morning one of the house fathers drove me to the Grayhound station in Marianna Florida. They left me there I was free most of my time was spent in thought of doing all the things that I had been dreaming of while locked up in boy school. I was a teenager who was swollen up with un-necessary pride an attitude that would lead me down the road of trouble, drugs, and prisons. I even thought I had my freedom, but I didn't understand the importance of it or its meaning at the time.

My mother and oldest sister Lynn was waiting for me when I arrived in St. Petersburg on our way home my mother explained to me all the changes that had happen since I've been away. The empty room in the front part of our house which was called the Florida porch would be my room. After putting away what little items I had accumulated I ask my middle sister Maxine if she could take me to my brothers Van and Donald's house.

After putting my things in my room Lynn and I took a walk to my brother's place. We knocked on the door several times then waited. When the door was opened it was my brother Van, he gave me a brotherly hug and welcomed me into his place. I was impressed from what I saw there was no doubt from the layout that my brothers had made their way in the world. The place was comfortable and in style with the times.

We smoked some excellent weed and talked about what's been going on since I've been away. After our conversation, on the way out, Van told me that I was welcome to return to his place anytime. From that day forward I took advantage of his offer and made it a habit to go over to his place as much as possible. It was one of the only places that offered me the freedom that I had been denied and couldn't get at my father's house. I had been away a while, so it was time for a wolf to get back in touch with St. Petersburg again find my place in these streets.

This was the south, so I lived on the colored side of town. Naturally this is where I got my impression of the world from. Getting into the bars and night clubs was no problem for me at that time.

No one really asked for a I.D plus I always handled myself like a grown man. There were several establishments located on 22nd St. In the hood we called the area the deuces. There was the Red Rum a little hole in the wall spot. Then there was Fortunes a pool hall & bar. This was the place where drug dealers, hustlers, and every other element of the streets hung out at to do what they do. Everyone shot pool at night, but it was more of a club. You could dance to the music coming out of the juke box.

In my younger years I thought that those areas were the only places to be. However, as I ventured further out, I found out that there was more to St. Petersburg than just the clubs and bars in the hood. There were upscale disco clubs on the north side such as the Executive Lounge, the Mark5, the rest were less mentionable. Over the course of time, I developed a sensation for the energy of the streets and its ambiance like a 6th sense. Along with the atmosphere the energy of the people gave me something different almost euphoric. I was connected to an education that was beyond the basic schoolbook education. The streets had its on education. My teachers and mentors were the pimps, players, hustlers, and ballers.

I don't know if I said this already, but downtown St. Petersburg is where I got into the hustling game for real. It's where I acquired most of the sophisticated knowledge used in order to hustle successfully in the field that I had chosen, a world of diamond, rubies, emeralds, and sapphires. All the precious and semi-precious stones you could think of, platinum, gold, silver, antiquities and other items of that luxury.

The more I dealt with those items the more I would learn. I didn't have to rely on someone else's decisions about what I should get for what I was fencing and selling. I knew how to make my own appraisals and set my own asking prices. I knew professional trade secrets like what the 4 C's of diamond quality is. The universal method for assessing the quality of any diamond consisting of color, clarity, cut, and carat weight. I could eyeball the difference between semi and precious metals such as gold, silver, and platinum. I could even tell the difference between the real value between 18 or 24 karats the real gold value. I understood numismatics and learned from gurus in the study of currency collection, including coins, new or old.

I always dressed stylish, but I learned from years in the game that how I dressed was important. I was hip on what to wear during certain times of the day or night, and how to get fitted for particular events. I realized that information and knowledge was an important factor, so I sorted out an array of intellectual fragments. Reading absorbing all sorts of books while memorizing different subjects and disciplines. This allowed to me to reach into those intellectual pockets of the knowledge form the professionals and evoke meaningful conversation at the very social events that I would hustle my way in and out of like a wolf in the night.

# Growing up in St. Petersburg Florida

Now that I was back living with my two older brothers. I needed to make a living of course hustling was my forte. I knew that a majority of Florida businesses open around eight in the morning. So, I was up dressed and out the door by 7:30 am. I had to walk to get downtown, but it wasn't that far distant.

I'd get downtown about 8am that gave me enough time to get an eye on things. I'm walking around looking checking in different shops, and stores, with each observation I'm also waiting for that wolf sense that I often get when there was a good opportunity somewhere just calling me. Usually for me it would be right 9 time out of 10. Then it happened I got that feeling it was drawing me towards this particular shop one that had not yet been graced my wolfish presence.

I opened the door entered into an air condition atmosphere shop. I didn't hear the sound of a bell or any sort of warning to the occupants. When entered the establishment. The dimension of the place may be 20ft x 40ft. possibly larger. A distinguishing looking older man had come from the back of the shop to welcome me. As I'm walking to the front to where he's at, I'm making a mental observation of the exterior of the shop, its contents of jewelry, and other items of quality all that are visible from glass cases on the walls behind the counter.

The gentleman was dressed in a casual manner but kind of close to business attire. The watch he was wearing I knew was gold, he had on his ring hand pinky finger a men's horseshoe shaped diamond ring, on his left hand he sported a men's diamond cluster ring.

"Good morning" he said, I returned the salutation can I help you he asks, I'm just looking right now, I responded then I walked around viewing items in the display cases an on the wall. Excuse me sir ask can I see this ring in the display case.

He walked over to where I was, and without unlocking the case he slides the display case door open. That one I say pointing to the ring it was a beauty a tiger's eye with diamonds the price tag on it was $850. I gave the ring to him and asked to view other items in the display case throughout our encounter I had to take my voice up a level in order for him to hear what I was saying.

After discussing the price of some of the items in the display case. I went into my ploy which was to get him to talk about himself. Business owner he was very comfortable and happy to be talking about himself, is why he decided to open up this type of business as well as how long he's been living in ST. Petersburg. I on the other hand did more listening than talking and lots of smiling.

Then a customer walks into the shop and he excuses himself from me to attend to the customer. There I am un-attendant making a mental note of the beautiful jewelry, coins and other valuable items in unlocked display case. The owner was occupied, and he was in complete attention of the customer.

Five to ten minutes later the customer leaves and he returns to where I was we continued our conversation. A few minutes later I said goodbye. This shop would be my next hustle.

I returned to the shop the next day somewhat around the same time I enter the shop and said hello. He was sitting at the front counter I made my way to the front where he was at. Then I made an attempt to resume the same conversation that he and I had the day before. He kind of seemed to have forget who I was and the contents of our conversation, but the more talk he remembered. I purchased a gold trinket of minimal value this was just one of my many ways into my game. One, get in good with my mark two make the person comfortable enough to trust me so there'll let their guard down.

As the time I was there before I did have to speck slightly above the normal tone confirmation was made not only did, he has a hearing problem, but he was also somewhat forgetful. Those impairments that he displayed I figured in as more of a benefit for my plan. As I made my way home, I began making plans I knew where and what I was going to steal.

I did a few other hustles to substitute my income until I was ready to return back to the shop and make the big hustle. I think it was three days later that I returned. I enter the shop we went through the same procedures. I said hello he returned the salutation from there we reestablish our communication we talked about some of the events that had occurred since the last time I was there and then we chit-chat for a few minutes.

I picked up the red book from off the counter paned through it and I came up with a question about a certain coin that was pictured in the book he gave me. I then explanation, which was in reality just a ploy of mines to get him to once again relaxed and establish his trust in me. So, I let him do most of the talking and teaching all the while I was waiting and anticipating for someone to enter into the shop.

Then it happened a customer walked in off the street and into the shop like several times before it plays out the same way. The owner excuses himself goes over to attend the customer there, I was un-attendant I wasn't going to let this opportunity get away. I go into Wolf mode I walk over to the right front further side of the counter always keeping the two of them in my sight wolf ears listening eyes scanning.

Now that I knew the two of their positions, Methodically and without hesitation I quickly reached over the top of the counter quietly, slid open the display case door reached in retrieved what I had knew that I wanted the plastic coin tube container with an unknown quantity of gold Krugerrands! I put the container in my front pants pocket, slide the display case door closed. I had what I wanted it was time for me to leave. I made my way to the front exit on my way out I said to the owner that I would try to make it back to see him later on in the week bidding him a good day. I was out the door and making my get away heading down streets and avenues all with a sinister wolfish grin on my face getting further and further away from the shop.

I took the container from out of my front pocket to check the contents jackpot! Just what I wanted there were 10 gold South African Kurgans, the value of each coin was somewhere in the neighborhood of $300 to $400 with a total possible sale of $2500 to $4000 to the right fence. I knew that if I wanted to get somewhere close to that, I would have to return back to town. It might be risky I thought but I had to do what I had to do.

I went to one shop fabricated a story about a visiting friend of mine from out of town who had some South African gold Kurgans for sale. He was willing to sell them at a discount price because of his need for cash due to an unfortunate situation. The situation resulted in the loss of not only his wallet, but cash as well. I told them he doesn't have any other form of identification. It took me a couple of tries before I would finally meet someone that was willing to deal with the situation.

He told me to tell my friend to bring the coins to his shop hopefully an agreement could be made. I was happy but also cautious of what I might be getting into, it could very well be a set up. I left the shop headed across the street down to the next corner and waited. I watched the shop to see if he was true to his word or was he setting me up to be arrested by the cops. I waited 15 minutes, when the police didn't show I was comfortable with returning back.

It was time to do business I sold 5 of the 10 coins for a total of $1200 cash no paperwork, and no haggling. $1200 was a lot of cash to me I was eighteen it was the 70s a win for sure; win for all plus I know had a fence.

I went to the Hilton hotel which during that time was a top-rated hotel. I checked into the hotel for a day went to my room to relax for a while until the night then I was going to hit the scene. I woke up from my nap it was late evening I showered, got dressed, splash on some cologne picked out my afro headed out I stepped out into evening air to enjoy what the streets of the night life had in store for.

The warmth of the night air felt good upon my face as I made my way to the deuces. I could hear the sound of the music as I approached the club, I took a moment to view the crowd. The music coming out of the juke box made the atmosphere party ready. I made my way to the bar ordered a drink. As I waited for my drink to arrive, I noticed from the corner of my eye this one particular lady she was looking at me her eyes was sending me a message.

My drink arrived I went over to where she was and asked her name. Her name was Kim. I asked; "can I sit with her". She said "yes". The bartender came over, since I had the means I offered her a drink she said that she'll have whatever I'm drinking. I ordered another Bacardi's and coke with a twisted of lime. I would have to play my cards right if I was going to get this lovely thang to go to the hotel with me tonight.

I went into my Mack conversation everything was going smooth. After ordering another round of drinks the rhythm of the funky music got into her soul. She wanted to dance I accepted her invitation out on the floor. She swayed and moved her hips I wondered to myself if she can move the same way in bed! We danced to a few songs instead of returning back to the bar, we sat in one of the available booths. She sat as close as possible to me, and her body language spoke to me as her hand explored different parts of my body.

I ordered another drink or two, for the nightlife was ours so we partied on down. From kissing to slow dancing, we enjoyed our time together. Good times and plenty of fun had passed between the two of us. We found ourselves in the late hour it was time for me to make my move. I asked her what's her plans for the rest of the night? Her response was whatever I wanted to do she could dig it.

We step out into the night air stone loaded after we smoked a joint, I was feeling good. I hailed for a cab it was off to the hotel. She and I went to my hotel room once in the room we made ourselves comfortable. She sat on the bed, and I turned on the TV. When I sat next to her on the bed everything was going good from the conversation I mixed in between the flirting. Then we started kissing and touching. I laid her down on the bed, with my free hand I began exploring her sexy warm smooth body. Once I helped her out of her clothing there she laid in the bed in her panties!

I stood up admiring her body wolfishly. Giving me the opportunity to stripe down to my boxers this would be a night of different position. It was one hell of a night kissing, touching, sucking, and fucking until we feel asleep. When I awoke it was morning, so I fucked her again. When she finally went to the bathroom, I just watched her sexy naked body as she seemed to float her way to the bathroom. When she exited the bathroom, she had already showered and dressed. We said our goodbyes and I escorted her to the door. So, I then showered, dressed, and headed downstairs for a good country breakfast.

I had some fresh roasted coffee along with grits, eggs and country fat country ham steak. After breakfast I bounced out went to the lobby to pay my hotel bill. I left the hotel went to my brother Vans spot to change clothing. From there I went to the park to hang out for a while. That day I was hoping on hope to run across a few friends, but deep down my thoughts were really preoccupied with the future. It was at this point in my life I knew that I was heading into another direction I was passing my teenager years. I left the park and proceeded back downtown. I needed to get my hustle on. The few dollars that I had made from the first sale, plus along with the remaining five gold coins wasn't going to last forever. I had to get back on my grizzly.

Today I was on the hunt for a different store. I went about my procedures as usual, checking out looking for that opportunity. There was this one shop that caught my attention. I looked through the window to see what it had to offer. Behind the counter was an elderly looking man possible in his early sixties. So, I went in walk to the front and introduced myself went right into wolf mode.

"Hello, I'm a young man interested in becoming familiar in numismatics. Right now, I'm in the early stage of coin collecting and was hoping that you could help me in my quest with some guidance and understanding as to what coins should I buy to add to my collection. A coin that would be a good investment and that would increase in value quickly. He was more than elated to accommodate me with not only his teaching but was soon in the process of showing me several coins he had on display. I showed an interest in his guidance and promised him that I would return for more information. Hopefully by then I would have saved up enough money to possibly buy at least one coin.

I already had the money, I just needed to do the game right. A few days later I returned back to the shop I purchased one of the coins that I had been enquiring about for $150. All the while I was taking a mental photo of the shop and where certain items were. Now that I had spent money at his shop it was time for me to develop a rapport with him, so I went into some more conversation with always allowing him to do most of the talking, teaching me more about the business of numismatics. I was like a student to him, so he took pleasure in teaching me.

My game was working I left in the middle of being taught with him asking if I would return. I did several times by then he and I had established a friendly connection. He became my teacher, and I was his student. He requested that when I was in the shop to read some of the magazines on the subject in teaching. Often if and when I was in the area I'd stop by at his shop, open up the door just to say hello, or good morning to him he would always reciprocate. The situation was beginning to go in the direction that I hoped it would, but it was the situation that I noticed that drew me to this hustle. One day on my way out the shop I turned back around to see what the owner would. Do more than once he would walk to the back of the shop without even paying attention to notice if I had left his establishment. I was confident he trusts he and I had developed had been solidified. It was time for me to put the idea that I had in my hustling mind into action.

I was up and dressed by seven thirty I walked non-stop to the shop. I entered the shop and greeted him good morning. I re-inquired about this particular coin that I had been showing interest in. He got the coin and we talked about it and then I paid for it. I told the owner that I wasn't able to stay for our usual talk because I had some important business that I needed to take care of.

I said goodbye and walked at an easy pace. As I was headed towards the entrance door, I pushed open the door as if I was leaving but took a glance back over my shoulder. He did what I had hoped that he would do. He was heading to the back of the shop. I didn't leave, I stayed right where I was waiting in silence until he was in the back out of sight. When he didn't come from the back of the shop to the front counter, I knew that he thought I had left so the coast was clear.

I went into wolf mode with the precision of a Swiss clock. I ducked down went behind the counter began duck walking to the area where I knew there were thirty-five or more plastic envelopes pinned to a board. Each one contained a different domination of old paper money. I took one that contained a couple of 1928B two-dollar red seal bills, along with another one that held two one-dollar PMG 20 Martha 1886 silver certificates. I waited and listened to any sound that indicated the shop owner was coming to the front. Everything remained the same, so I continued hustling. Opening up the display case I removed a case of sixteen rings of various qualities and precious stones, along with a plastic coin holder that I knew contained ten 1884-cc Morgan BU silver dollars jackpot!

When I was satisfied with what I had, I made my way to the front entrance door and exited. I went to the fence that I had been dealing with in town. I sold him the paper money and coins. I was still only somewhat freshly taught in the knowledge of what I had, so I sold what I had for a couple of thousand dollars.

After I went back home to my brother's place chilled out laid low for the night. The next day I returned back to the shop that I had stolen the paper money and coins from. It was my way of removing any suspicions that it was me that did it. I was surprised that he didn't mention anything about, well anything! I believed that he had no knowledge that those items were even gone.

I waited a couple of weeks before I did the same thing again, but I still spent time there with him. We talked; as well I received an education into a better understanding of coins. But of all the important things I learned about getting inside, around, or into these types of people is one thing. It was something I would be encountering in that environment as long as I was in Florida. I was hustling in as a black man in the south. Hustling in what was at that time strictly a white man's business. So, looking a certain way was important to the game, I started investing some of my earnings into my appearance to help draw the attention away from myself, so as to blend in with the tourists, everyday jewelers, and business men.

I did my shopping at Mass Brothers and up north clothing broker that was down here in Florida. They had all the necessities such as suits, dress shirts and ties, cuff links, and tie clips. But for my urban look I got my clothing at Mr. Mans. I used stolen jewelry for trade so that I had attractive jewelry.

As the months turned into years, I was doing good in the hustling game, but I was still living with my brothers. This was alright but before venturing out on my own I felt that there was so much more that I needed to learn before going out into the jungle. When that time came, I wanted to be as close to ready as possible, knowing that once I take that step, I would be out there on my own in the jungle of the streets.

My brothers' choice of business would have them spending most of their time at the Three Oaks Lounge and hotel. It was owned by the same drug supplier that they worked for. If you were a player or someone in the game this was one of the hippest places to be. Both of my brothers each had Lincoln Continentals, the ones with suicide doors. As for me I drove around in a rental car for some time until I had enough money to buy my car. It was a Buick Wildcat. The top was white with a gold body. I pimped it out by putting a silver flying lady on the front of the hood, and two-inch gangster white wall tires with spinner rims, and a complete eight track sound system.

It was all about the hustle and going to every possible place I could get paid like the day at the mall. There I was looking and going from store to store then I saw it, my opportunity. I went into wolf mode I noticed one employee working this jewelry store but wasn't sure. It was like that all the time, so I made a mental note of it. I returned several times to the mall. The situation was always the same and so I began to keep track of the time and plot out my plan.

I went back to the mall the following week at the same time walked past the jewelers to see if the situation would be the same and it was. I didn't go into the store but made a mental note of the dimensions of the store. It was square shaped with a wall down the center, which made it actually two sided. There was one entrance which was closer to the left side of the store. I knew what I had to do.

I returned the next day and waited just outside the door for the right opportunity. The moment came when a man accompanied by a female friend went into the shop. I made my move coming in right behind them and quickly going over to the other side of the store. The couple didn't even notice or feel me as I slipped into the store behind them. I waited on the other side in silence, nothing. I made a quick peek around the partition of the store and the salesman was busy trying to make a sale to the customers. No one knew I was in the store.

I went into hustle mode quiet as possible my adrenaline was flowing on a high, with my eyes, body, feet, and soul all in harmony like a wolf making my way towards my prey. Quickly I went behind the counter. It was unlocked! All the while I'm watching looking for shadows and listening at the same time as I reached inside the display case and grabbed tray after tray!!! I stuck them one by one into pillowcases sewed into the lining of my jacket. It all happened smoothly like a movie playing out and I was the star Al Monday.

That was enough. I knew that I didn't have much time. It was time for me to leave so I peeked around the partition to see what my options were, and the salesman was still busy trying to make that sale. I kept my eyes on them as I slowly and quietly slipped out the door like the wind into the traffic of people moving within the mall.

There was no time to stop or check what's behind me as I exited the mall and went straight to my car. I kept it smooth and drove within the speed limits until I believed I was a good distant away from the mall. I parked in a noticeable, but unnoticeable area. I retrieved the trays from the pillowcase in my jacket. Some of the rings had fallen out into the pillowcase. After collecting them and placing them in the ring tray, what a beautiful sight.

Two trays had all types of lady's rings with diamonds, rubies, and emeralds. The third tray was men's diamond rings of all characters and clusters, others had a single stone. This was at that time one of the best scores I had made. A smile graced my face as I did mental addition of the money that I would get. I put everything in a bag and made my way back to St. Pete.

The first stop I made would be my brothers' place. He was home we sat and smoked a joint down as I told him the story. I pulled out all the trays from the bag and showed him the rings. He looked them over and made me an offer for two ladies, and one men's diamond ring. I gave him the family discount of $500 each ring. In total I started with forty-eight rings minus two that I sold to my brother, and I kept three for myself. I didn't want to sell all of them at one time so I put ten of them in hiding for later, the rest I would sell.

I changed my clothing and headed downtown being careful as I made my way through the streets and avenues to my fence. He was in I showed him all the rings. He tried to hide the fact, however, I could see the excitement hidden behind his eyes that he knew the rings were extremely valuable. He did his usual examination through the jeweler's eye.

I knew that I had over $28,000 in jewels. I waited for his offer. He offered me $6,500 and I asked for $12,000. We agreed on $8,500. Adding the $500 I got from my brother altogether I made $9,000. That was a lot of money for a young man in his teens during the 70's. Life was good.

I gave my brother $2,000 because I was living at his place. From then I decided to take some time off from hustling and enjoy my bounty. Thursday nights there was music and dancing at the Bartley Park recreation center. I was going to be as fly as super fly at the dance. I drove downtown to Mr. Man, a high-quality fashion relatively expensive store. It was said that the shoes and clothing line he sold was from New York. It was the 70's so I purchased a pair of knee-high silk socks, platform shoes, bell bottom pants, silk shirts with and without patterns, and added jumpsuits for a later time. I even added some flare to my style and brought a black cane with an ivory handle that had a hidden knife.

After that I headed back to the apartment to rest up a bit. I awakened around six-thirty, time to get ready. I showered, dried off and got dressed. I was looking fly, the finally touch a slight spray of afro sheen, picked out my afro and proceeded to head outdoors. I looked at myself in the mirror on the way out the door. There was no way that I wasn't going to score.

I got in my car and drove to the dance. I parked, lit up a joint and smoked a bone. A few minutes later I was ready. I got out of the car and made my way to the dance. Once inside I walked around to see what the crowd was like, and to also give the young ladies a look at me. I located a spot to lean with my hands over my cane Mack styling while I chilled and checked out the honeys.

The music was bumping to the sound of the 70's and I was enjoying the music and my high. Across the floor standing by herself was a fine little brown bone. I was about to make my move when I felt a tap on my shoulder. I turned around to see who it was. I didn't recognize him, but he knew me. He points towards these two fine girls tells me that he already knew one of them, that he had sex with her and wanted to get back with her. But she was with her partner. He suggested that him and I hook up with them so I'm thinking cool this might be easy. We make our way across the dance floor I introduced myself to the girl that he overlooked.

"What's happening baby?" I asked her. "Are you here by yourself?" She said that she was with her friend, but not a boyfriend. "Cool," I said and introduced myself. "You want to dance?"

We went out on the floor and danced. She was a good dancer we danced to a few songs then I escorted her off the floor. "Say, you smoke?" I asked her. She did. "You want to go out to my car and smoke a joint with me?" I made small conversation as we went to the car. I unlocked the door then held it open for her. She got in sat down, I closed the door went around to the driver's side let myself in and sat in the car. We smoked a joint while drinking some Boones Farm strawberry hill wine.

I was feeling good as we made our way back into the dance. It was perfect as we entered the lights went low it was time to slow dance. I took her out on the dance floor and took control. We danced as if we were having sex with our clothes on. The way she responded I had a feeling that her and I would be fucking tonight.

It was ten o'clock the dance was coming to an end. She told me that she was going to look for her friend, to tell her that I will be taking her home tonight. I asked her to meet me back at my car. I ran back into the guy that had showed me the girls. He was still in the company of the girl that he claimed he already had sex with. I pulled him to the side away from the girl he was with then asked him what his plan with the other girl was. Me and my girl are going back to my place to listen to some music, smoke some weed, and drink some more wine. You know keep the party going on. "Never know what might happen", I said in a way that he had to know what I was suggesting. You and your lady friend are invited to go with us.

I looked around for the girl I had been with then just decided to go to my car. Sure, enough there she was waiting ready like a muthafucka! Everyone got in the car, the girl I was with sat in the front seat next to me, while the other girl sat with the guy in the back seat. I didn't have far to go as I lived close to the park. Once there I parked the car everyone got out and followed me to the cottage.

Once inside everyone sat down, the mood was halfway set as the black light was reflecting off the posters on the walls, while the psychedelic light was spinning its colors. I turned on the stereo and stacked the albums for play- Rick James, Earth Wind and Fire, some Islay Brothers, followed by some smooth Barry White. Both girls sat next to each other on the couch. I sat at the table rolled a joint, passed it to the girls, then went to the kitchen to get a bottle of Boone's Farms strawberry hill.

When I returned, I sat the bottle down with some glasses so everyone could help themselves. I turned my attention to the girl I was with and asked her if she knows how to braid.

"Sure," she said.

"Can you braid my hair?" She pointed towards herself, and then asked me to sit down between her legs. I jump up real quick went to get the combs and hair grease then shot right back so she could start braiding my hair. When I returned, she had already poured two cups of wine one for me and the other for her. I gave her the combs and hair grease and sat down between her legs as the joint made its way around. The music was playing, the weed was being passed, and ever thing was right.

The other guy took things into his own hands, I was cool with that. He took her to the other room. Since he told me that he had fucked her before, him getting into those panties again should be no problem. Or so I thought! I'm relaxing in my high, she's braiding my afro, then I heard banging on the opposite side of the wall along with the muffling sound of the girl's voice. Something was wrong.

I immediately get up and rushed into the bedroom. He's on top of her holding his hand over her month. I could see the look of horror in her eyes. I reached over the bed and grabbed the guy right off of her, she jumps up and runs into the living room with her friend. I tell the guy, "Man, you got to get the fuck out of my house now!"

I'm shoved him towards the door out he goes. I got to calm this chick down. I'm thinking about my reputation, or her telling her parents and the police get involved in everything. I apologized to her, told her that the guy told me that they knew each other and had you already been together. She says to me that she thought that he was a friend of mine as that's what he told her, it was the only reason she agreed to come back to the crib with him.

That's when my brother Van walks into the apartment. I tell him what happened, and he takes over and they leave. I go back to getting my hair braided. The mood had been interrupted but things got back on track as chocolate girl and I make our way to the bedroom, and I did what any fucksmen does. I hunted that fox down and waxed that ass.

I sold the last of the rings I had for $2,300 and continued living the high life but when your young money goes fast. My time away from the hustling game was coming to an end. With all that I was doing it was time to get back into the game. I was changing my character, my style was becoming that of a mature man. So, I stopped going to those jitterbug dances or hanging at the park.

My brothers told me about two places to go: the Executive Lounge, and the Mark Five. Despite the fact that I was 17 my appearance, the way that I carried myself said I was older. I was always ready and confident as I stepped into the Executive Lounge for the first time. The atmosphere was refreshing for the first time I was in a club with a mixer of white, and black people. This was different from what I had been around I was far beyond the hood.

It was time for me to see if I had matured in my game. I knew that I would fit somewhere in between especially with the plan I had in mind this was the perfect spot. There was a dance floor the music was more on the smooth tempo with a mixture of R&B and disco. I made my way to the lounge to eye hunt the ladies. Most of them were white so this would be different, but I knew they had money and I had been taught by one of the best players, my brother Van. His philosophy was anyone can get pussy, but only the best players get paid. This was my night to see if I had the skills. I was admiring the ladies sitting at the bar and happen to notice this one particular lady giving me inviting eyes paying close attention to me as I was making my way around the club. I could tell that she was interested in me.

I sauntered past her to see what response I would get, when I did, she felt comfortable enough to reach out and put her hand on my arm. She held on to my arm holding up my progress, at the same moment asking me my name. I introduced myself she asked me if I wanted a drink. Rum and coke with a twist of lime I said. Her name was Debbie, we indulged in conversation as we waited for our drinks. When they arrived she paid for them.

I kept her entertained I had her laughing and smiling the whole time. After we finished our drinks, she called the bar tender over and ordered us another round. Things were going really good; the music was jamming so we danced a few times, after the third round of drinks she whispered in my ear that she had a secret to tell me. I told her that her secret would be safe with me. She told me that she had a boyfriend who was a weed dealer. To me this meant that if I played it right, I could have a lady friend who can supply me with as much weed as I want to for free.

I wasn't about to blow this possibility. I maintained my composure and acted as if what she told me wasn't important. I grabbed her delicately by her hand took her onto the dance floor. We danced to a few more records, then the DJ put on a slow jam; New Birth "Been such a long time." I pulled her close to my body in a tender but manly manner. She gave in to the closeness of my touch as we slow danced. I slowly grinded on her body as if I was making love. I made sure that she felt the semi-hardness of my dick against her pussy and from her response I knew that she wanted something more than just a slow dance from me.

The song ended and I escorted her back to the bar where she ordered our drinks and paid for them. Throughout our conversation she was concerned more with my body, exploring with her fingers my chest and arms. She then moved in for a kiss. I responded appropriately to her advances. I knew what I had to do if it was going to work in my benefit.

We danced a few more times, but it was the last slow song that made me understand that tonight she was going to be mines. She pulled me very close to her body and she danced as if she was in the bed with me. It was time to leave. I told her that I had a wonderful night and I hoped that she did to, but I need to leave so that I can get to the other side of town where I live. She grabbed ahold of my arm and told me that I didn't have to walk; she would give me a ride to wherever I needed to go.

That was what I wanted to hear. I stayed a little longer we danced and partied until the closing hour. We exited the club and walked to her car in the parking lot. She looked at me and says that she's too high to drive and suggested that we get a room. We didn't have to go far as there was a hotel next to the club. I waited outside as she went in the lobby to fill out the paperwork. Once inside the hotel room I sat on the bed she excused herself and went to the bathroom.

I heard the shower, so I undressed and turned off the lights turned on the TV. When she came out of the bathroom, I was lying underneath the sheets in my boxers waiting for her to join me. I could see the silhouette of her body. She allowed the towel to fall from her body while making her way to the bed, laying down on her back. I began kissing her. Our lips touched in a passion; my hand travelled down her soft lovely body making my way to her garden between her thighs. I began rubbing her clit with my middle finger she became aroused and wet.

My lips moved from her lips to the erect nipples of her breasts, a little more foreplay until I knew that she was ready. I stood up and remove my boxers revealing my big hard dick. A look of pleasure graced her lips, the gleam in her eyes told a story. I climbed back into bed on top of her body. Slowly I penetrated her putting every inch of my dick up into her warm and wet pussy. She moaned with satisfaction and pleasure. I kissed her lips around her neck down to her breast. As my mouth sucked her pink nipples, she moaned her body moved with desire.

Fifteen to twenty minutes of fucking and then I can tell from the change of sound, that she's making that she was about to come, pulling me closer, and closer to her, wanting every inch of my dick, begging me, "fuck me baby fuck me" she kept saying, then like a river she exploded all on my dick! I was still high on the rum and coke and that would keep me from busting my nut. I rode that pussy all through the night until she came two more times, she laid on my chest and we fell asleep. I watched T V until I drifted off to sleep.

In the morning I fucked her once again. She came and I busted a hard nut into her pussy. After taking a shower together we dressed and left to go have breakfast. Eggs, grits, bacon and coffee. After breakfast I told her to drop me off at Berlet Park. As we parted, she handed me a piece of paper with her phone number written on it and told me to please call her anytime.

That relationship lasted about four to six months. I did my very best to get what I could before it ended. Some of the best things about being with her was that she always was on time with the bud. Whenever we got together, she understood my needs getting money from her was no problem. As long as I gave her the entire dick, along with a good time, that she could handle.

The money that I was getting from her was just a part of my hustles. I didn't rely on just that. I was still hustling downtown. That brings us to that unfortunate day. One evening as I was hustling looking for that money opportunity, I decided to go into this department store. I made the mistake and disregarded my warning censor. I was to wrapped up in the money, when knowing damn well all money is not good money.

The thing about it was I had been stealing items from this store for some time now and had never got caught. I'm walking around in the store behind the counter were five very expensive cameras. All I saw was dollar signs it was too easy to pass up. I looked around, didn't see a floor walker, or anyone that looked as if there were watching me. I went behind the counter, gathered all of the cameras then put them in one of the large bags already behind the counter.

On my way out the door a couple of security workers stopped me I was busted. The police were called they hauled my ass to the juvenile center. It was back to Arthur G. Dozier School for Boys for me. It was as if I didn't leave. It was the same old song since I knew most of the guys that were there, I graduated with no problem, making my stay short as possible. When I was released, I returned home things had changed. Donald had moved in with this chick and was out of the drug game. Van was still living the bachelor life. I knew that I couldn't live at my father's house, so I moved in with him. I went back to what I had been doing in order to pull my weight. I knew that it was a risky lifestyle, but it was all that I knew. I was seventeen. A year or so had gone by mastering my craft and learning more about the world I was hustling in.

# County Jail Gail and Drugs

I can't remember exactly what I was arrested for, but it had to be something minor because I did 90 days. I also was able to work as one of the jailhouse trustees, which allowed me somewhat of a free run within the building. One day as I was sweeping the catwalk on the female side one of the female inmates was sitting on the bunk.

I said hello to her. It looked as if she was not feeling well. she asked me if I had something sweet. I said yes it would for sure make her feel better as well. She had a pretty face but that was all I could see of her at that time. Her name was Gail. I explained to her that I did not have any candy on me right now. But if she could hang on until I am finished with what I am doing I would return later with some candy. It did not take me long to do my job that day. I wanted to get back to her as soon as I could. I stopped at the lobby store, paid for a couple of Charleston Chew candy bars then headed back upstairs down the catwalk to the cell.

I handed her the two bars of candy. She asked me my name then asked how much time I was doing. "60 days", I told her. She was doing 30 days. We didn't go into much detail about one another's reason for being locked up. I could not stay as long as I would have wanted to. So, I told her that I'd be back tomorrow. I thought about Gail throughout the night.

The next day I couldn't wait to see her. As the weeks went by, we developed a friendly relationship. That was when she finally felt comfortable enough to tell me what she was doing in jail. Gail was a lady of the night, a professional lady of the night no vampire either. That's how she made her money. Me being a part of the elements in the streets I understood and accepted it.

It was my growing year's curiosity that fascinated me. She was beautiful, sexy, oh my gawd she had the biggest tits I had ever seen too. Gail was originally from NY. That along with her experience in the profession gave her the upper hand. It was that hand that would teach me a young man many lessons. Some of them could be considered not good, but they were all lessons in strengthening me for the journey I would take in my life.

She was always talking about the money that she was making, but she was out there in the streets on her own. As she got closer to her release date, she came to me with a proposition if I wanted to be her man, ya know watch her back as she's out there making money. I explained to Gail that I knew very little about the pimping game. She explained to me that all I had to do was collect the money that she made from tricking. That seemed easy, but in reality, all I really wanted to do was to fuck her. I was young so as a young man I was thinking with my dick. We made plans to reunite at Cameo, a club on Central Avenue. Gail completed what little time she had to do and left. I thought about her from the day she left could not wait to see her again.

As a trustee I was required to do what was asked of me. I never thought it would be cleaning the evidence room. I was cleaning the tier when one of the guards asked me to go with him to do some extra cleaning. I had to clean and sweep several offices. One of those offices happened to be the evidence room.

There I was cleaning the evidence room where there were ten to twenty shelves of all kinds of shit! My Wolf senses where doing cartwheels, backflips every day I had to go in there. On those shelves were yellow envelopes as well as other items, boxes, bags you know what u would think would see in an evidence room. The larceny in me was awakened like a Werewolf busting out. What the fuck could be in those envelopes? I did what I had been doing just about up to this point of my life. I am cleaning at the same time keeping a watch on the jailer. As soon as I noticed that he wasn't paying attention to me as good as he should have been. I went into Alpha mode.

In one single motion as I'm sweeping the floor, I swing the broom sweep three, maybe four yellow envelopes off the shelves mixing them in with the trash. Off into the waste barrel that I had. The jailer saw nothing. After completing my work for that day, it was time to take the trash bags out to be picked up the next day. I double tied the trash bag that had the yellow envelopes. I marked it with a strip of a small white rag so it would be easily recognizable.

I set all the trash bags outside next to a large metal container then went inside to make a call from the police lobby to my brother Van. When he answered the phone, I told him that I needed him to do me a favor. I explained to him what to look for and where. There was nothing more that I could do, but Van being my brother I knew that was all I had to do. I returned to my cell to watch from the window.

In the evening night I saw the lights of a car. It slowed down then parked. It was my brother. I watched as he cautiously made its way towards the dumpster retrieving the bag. Then returning to his car driving away. The next day I called my brother. He had the bag, but I would have to wait until I was released to know the contents of those envelopes which was not far ahead. I went about doing my job.

That date arrived my 90-day sentence was completed. It was time for me to be released. I had business to take care of knowing the contents of those yellow envelopes was top priority. My date with Gail was also a top priority as well. When I arrived at Van's as always music was coming from within the apartment. I knocked on the door but got no answer, so I knocked again. He finally big bro came to the door, we slapped five along with what the traditional what's happening greeting. Once inside I made myself comfortable on the living room couch. The smell of weed was in the air, as well as out on an album cover my brother had been deseeding.

I rolled a dobie while my brother went into the bedroom. When he returned he was carrying a small bag. He hands it to me tells me that this is what is left of the items from the yellow envelopes. I maintained my cool. I lit up the joint, took a few pulls then passed it to him. I opened the bag inside was a small black bag. I unzipped it the contents consisted of a glass syringe with extra needles. I zipped the bag closed placing it to the side. What else was in there?

There was a white envelope. I opened it up to see some money that made me smile. Van told me it was my cut from the sale of cocaine and heroin that were in some of the envelopes. I think it was a month, maybe sooner but the police noticed the missing evidence from the evidence room. After putting one and two together. I was arrested then charged with theft, but when the case went before the court the judge told the D A that the police department was negligent for putting me a situation like the evidence room. What did they expect for me to do? Plus, there was no evidence pointing directly to me as being the one that committed the theft. Nothing became of it they had no other choice but to release me.

Anyway, rewind back a little. Before all that bullshit happened as me and bro are smoking weed getting high catching up on the street life. I told Van about meeting Gail and our plans. He told me to make sure that I followed up on that money. I took a moment to chill in my high enjoying the moment in the soul funk of the music. Later on, that evening after taking a shower I changed into platform shoes with bell bottom pants. I was ready for my first night with Gail.

I called a cab. Cameo I said. I stepped into the Cameo and stood in the doorway like I was the Mack and Super Fly all in one, taking a moment to feel and absorb the atmosphere. It was in coordination with my style and the times. I looked around for Gail. She was at the bar with other ladies of the night entertaining and wetting their whistle off the tricks, all of them hoping that they had enough money to find pleasure in one of their arms. Gail was dressed in a pair of tight white-hot pants that seemed to have been put on with a paint brush. She had a nice ass, proudly displaying her big bosoms in a red halter top. She turned around for whatever reason. I was elated that she remembered me. In an extraordinary display of talent, she walked in my direction, called me daddy pulled out a wad of cash from her halter top then handed it to me. "This is for you," she said.

I was a freshman at this pimping game, but at that moment I was on the right avenue. Little did I know that this would be the beginning of something I knew nothing about, but I played my position. She invited me up to the bar for a drink, then she introduced me to the other ladies as her pimp. I ordered my usual Bacardi and coke with a twist of lime. In the process of waiting for my drink, we discussed my position in this affair in comparison to her responsibilities, so everything was understood. All throughout the night Gail was in and out with different men.

It was getting late the customers were few. Gail informed me that it was time to call it a night. Gail called a cab, an old reliable trick that she knew that runs cabs for her. This would be our ride to her place. As were riding I couldn't help but to notice Gail didn't have to tell him where to go, he already knew the routine. He made a stop, I thought this was her apartment until she asked me to wait in the cab until she gets back.

As I waited for her to return the cab driver and I talked. I understood the relationship between him and Gail. He was nothing more than a trick, another John. Five to 10 minutes had pasted when Gail returned to the cab her personality and the mood was noticeable different to me. I had no idea that she was under the hoof of the white horse of heroin. Nothing was spoken as the cab drove to our destination. All the while she lay comfortable on my chest with my arms around her.

We finally pulled up to a large house. No money was exchanged between Gail and the driver just a hidden understanding. When we got inside of the house it was a rooming house. Most if not all the occupants were females, most of which I had seen or encountered this night at the Cameo. I followed Gail down the hallway to her room and along the way I took notice that the house did have a good size kitchen, a dining and a living room.

She unlocked the door, turned on the small bedside light. It was of low wattage, making the atmosphere mellow. I sat down on the bed, to turn on the radio. It was already set on WTMP, a black station broadcasting out of Tampa, Florida. Gail grabbed a towel and whatever she needed then excused herself. She made her way down the hall to what was the shower room to wash off the nightlife.

I counted the cash that Gail had made. There was $4000 and this would be her quota. I heard the sound of her footsteps as she made her way back to the room. The scent of her perfume filled the air when she walked into the room. She removed the towel and revealed some sexy lingerie. Just like I thought she was sexy fine.

She went into the closet and handed me a towel and a face cloth along with a bar of soap in a soap dish. The shower was at the end of the hallway.

She said, "don't forget to bring the soap back".

I smiled. After my quick shower when I entered the bedroom Gail was laying on the bed looking caramel sexy in a sexy negligee. Those big breasts, the nipples were erect and inviting. She was definitely a beauty from New York City and tonight I was going to take pleasure in all of it.

Tonight, was going to be something special knowing I had been with teenage girls, but Gail was a 24-year-old well-developed woman with experiences of the street. I would learn one of her secrets, she would also teach me something new in what it meant to satisfy a woman. I sat down on the bed, towel still wrapped around my waist. Gail slid over and laid her head on my thigh. The sound of the smooth music was playing in the background.

I looked into her beautiful brown eyes then kissed her luscious lips. She smiled turning rolling over onto her side. Reaching over she retrieved two needles that she had prepared for us. I was lost, the way she was dressed and everything. I knew what she was, if I wanted to be with this fine sexy goddess then I was willing to go along with what she wanted me to do.

This would be my introduction into the world of Heroin. She spoke with the talent of her profession, a voice sweet and intoxicating I was unable to resist so when she asked me to hold out my arm I complied. I felt the sting of the needle as it pierced my skin the warmth of the drug surging into my vein, and throughout my body the sensation of the king heroin took over my body. She booted it a few times and removed the needle. It was my first shot of dope, but it would not be my last.

I laid back on the pillows absorbed in my new high as she did her shot. We lay in the bed for a while. I felt her hands touch my chest then the warmth of her tongue kissing her way to my mouth passionately inviting me to return the passion. Her desires as well as my wants became one. It was here the moment that I had been dreaming and waiting for was now mine for the night. Exploring this goddess before me was like heaven. Her firm but soft body was all that I thought it would be.

She began kissing and touching my body, undoing the towel around my waist. I laid back and enjoyed the warmth of her month. She was a master with what she was doing to my hard erect dick. The pleasure and joy I received was something that I had not experienced. She stopped and climbed on top guiding my extremely hard manhood into her warm and wet pussy, slowly taking ever inch. She moaned and groaned with passion moving in a smooth rhythm. I reached up to undo the strings of her negligee revealing her big and beautiful breasts fondling her nipples. She's leaned over so that I can enjoy the pleasure of her sweet erect nipples. The chemistry of sex I could smell coming in the night air.

She climbed off and laid in the bed. I climbed on top of her kissing everywhere possible- lips, ear and around her neck to each nipple. When I went down and kissed her on the belly button, she gently put her hands on top of my head coaching me to continue my journey down, down to her garden. The fragrance captivated me. I couldn't resist and began to taste the sweet nectar with my tongue exploring every part of her sweet and lovely pussy in search of the fruits that were ripening in her garden.

She touched her clit with her finger, I knew that was where she wanted me to venture. Her clit rose as did the moans. As her breathing increased, she started to move intensively holding my head in its position she let out this scream from deep within as her body moved intently until she slowly settled into the comfort of the bed motionless with a smile of sunshine upon her face. She kissed me and we laid in the bed for a minute.

She reached over and grabbed my hard dick. I climbed on top of her. My dick was still in her hand as she guided it home inside her warm and wet pussy. Our rhythm was slow as we fucked round and round, in and out, up and down. She was experienced unlike any female that I ever had sex with. I did my best, but she was fucking me. I could tell that something was happening.

I was hooked but I had to learn from that to be able to move forward. I was young and I was in another part of the game taking steps moving up in the world of manhood. The darkness of drugs, hustling as the game presented itself.

I awakened to the morning of another day. It was time for me to roll into another part of the life. Gail cooked bacon, scrambled eggs and grits for breakfast. During breakfast Gail explained to me my role. I was to meet her later on that day at Cameo she would have my money. I headed back to the apartment. My brother Van was there. I explained to him the events that had occurred to get his knowledge of the situation and how I should handle it.

After being schooled by him I knew what it was that I had to do. I hadn't mentioned the drug usages. Days turned into weeks and weeks into months. After spending so much of our time together getting high and fucking, we decided to live together so I moved in with her. Still hustling throughout the day downtown but at night I was at the Cameo with Gail as she got my money.

I was meeting and getting to know the other ladies of the night at the Cameo as well. In time I was chosen by two other ladies, but I considered Gail as my front and top lady. She did her job as expected. Other than having the girls work at Cameo every so often, especially on the weekend, I'd take them all to work on 22nd Street, known to those in the life as the Deuces. That's where players, pimps, hustlers, drugs dealers and junkies hung out. I had enough money coming in from various hustles, so I decided to rent a car, but I didn't have a driver's license. So, I had my brother Van rent a car for me. With transportation I added another element to my various hustles boosting (Shoplifting).

It was a sunny Florida day, a good a day as ever to take the ladies to the mall to get them in the boosting game. We headed out to the mall in the car. I parked in the lot leaving the car unlocked just in case one of my ladies needed to hide, or if we needed to make a quick getaway.

So, there we are me and my three ladies going in the mall, as were walking casing out different stores something caught my wolf senses. I noticed an older white male over fifty in a jewelry store, to me it looked as if he was there by himself. I made note of the time and to give that situation more attention I sent the ladies to go do what they do.

I hung around the jewelry store getting information to be used at another time. My ladies met up with me later it was a successful day. As we made our way back to the hood, I explained to them about the store situation and my plan which involved all of them. The next day we headed back to the mall to execute my plan. I waited outside in the mall corridor across from the jewelry store watching as my three ladies all dressed in sexy looking outfits entered. They used flirtation along with revealing just enough of their body goods as a distraction on the older guy. I could see that my plan was working.

It was time for phase two of my part. I slipped into the shop as the ladies kept the man preoccupied enabling me to enter un-noticed and un-heard. The jewelry store had two sides with a door sized entrance to the other I was on that side of the store, just me. The beauty of all the diamonds, rubies, and sapphires set in their rings was all for the taking. I smiled a wolfish grin to myself.

All the display cases were locked, but I came prepared for that. I pulled out my trusty pearl handle silver knife and slipped it in between the wedges of the top glass of the display case. There was no glue to hold the glass to the counter so there was no problem lifting the glass with my free hand. I used a handkerchief for two reasons- to hold the glass and to leave no fingerprints. I grabbed three cases of diamond rings putting them into my pockets and slowly lowered the glass back into place.

I peeped around the opening to the other side of the store where my girls still had the guy smiling keeping his attention. I exited the same way I had entered walked to the car then waited for my girls. They arrived in less than two minutes. We headed back to the hood. I blessed each girl with a ring of my choice but gave Gail four beautiful ladies rings. I had one priority, finding a buyer. I was familiar with the thread in the fabric of the streets. I knew that Geechee Dan was the man to see. I dropped my ladies off at Cameo to continue their job and I left in search of the Geechee Dan man.

I drove to the Deuces, parked in the parking lot then asked if anyone had seen Geechee Dan. The word was that he was somewhere on the Deuces. I went to Fortunoes, and I walked in sitting at the bar was Geechee. I walked up to him asked him if he would be interested in buying some rings. I told him that I had some diamond rings for sale. That seemed to catch his attention.

"Show me what you have," he said.

I turn inwards towards him so that no one could see our business. I showed him a couple of diamond rings still with the high price tag on them. So, he asked what I wanted for all of them.

"$11,000 I said".

He counter offered, "I'll give you $8,000."

Wanting to get them out of my possession I agreed

. "Alright," I said.

"Meet me across the street in the parking lot in thirty minutes," he said.

I sat at the bar ordered a beer. The music occupied my time, but that thirty minutes it felt like an hour. I shot a couple games of pool then went outside to check. In five no more than ten minutes he pulled up in his car parking it in the parking lot. I hurried across the street to where he was parked.

"Get in the back seat," he says.

There was some guy in the back seat that I had never seen before. I didn't mind being that I was in the company of someone with a good reputation. Geechee asked me if I don't mind if his associate took a look at all the rings. Geechee drove around as me and his associate sat in the back seat of the car. His associate looked at the rings through a jeweler lope in comparison to the price tag that was on every ring.

With every look he smiled and nodded his head in a positive manner. When he completed his appraisal, he gave it the seal of approval. Product and money were exchanged.

"Here you go $8,000 in a white envelope."
I fanned the bills within the envelope, it looked to me as if it was $8,000. He drove me back to the parking lot. I got out and watched as his car drove away. Once inside of my car I took the money out the envelope and counted, it was $8,000.

From there I drove to the Three Oaks Club to see if my brother Van was there, but he wasn't so I drove back to Center Street to the Cameo and picked up my ladies. "Let's go girls," I said to Gail. She handed me what money had been made while I was away. "Ladies, it is time to upgrade."

With everyone in the car I drove to the north side 45<sup>th</sup> street. The Cheyenne Social club a hotel/night club. This would be our place of residence. I rented a double room a month at a time. I was living large if any ask how I was doing I said, "Sitting in the shade drinking cold lemonade reading the funnies and counting my mother fucking money." It also offered a more productive opportunity for my ladies to work. As this place had an upscale environment and clientele. I didn't have to say it. They knew what must be done to work the hotel lobby and lounge during the day and the club during the night.

I was young but doing it like the big boys. The word got around about the lifestyle that I was living. I had set a new standard in the game in the city of St. Petersburg. Most of St. Petersburg hustlers, pimps and players tried to emulate me but none could duplicate it. Even thought I had $8,000 that didn't stop me from hustling. I was still doing my thing stealing and selling jewelry and gold coins. I was very proud of my accomplishments. When my brothers Van and Duck would come visit me at the new place, I was calling home, we would sit out by the pool in the shade drinking strawberry daiquiris. Laughing and kicking about the game of the events occurring in our life. At that moment I thought I was unstoppable.

# Cocaine and STEELHEAD

Being in the life making the kind of money that I was making certain things came into play. As for me it would be (cocaine) or as it was referred to during my time girl. I was shooting up heroin, but not every day so I didn't have a heroin habit. I was more concerned with making money and my girls.

It was a Friday evening, and I was having another one of my social parties at the hotel. My guests included hustlers, players, pimps and hoes. The music was playing drinks of all kinds were flowing and cocaine was on the table. I was indulging myself in a sniff when I heard a commanding voice say, "Why are you wasting your money sniffing cocaine? It was a player named Steelhead. My head rose up from the plate after doing a line of cocaine. I think it was the drug, but it looked to me as if he was addressing that statement directly at me.

I didn't respond to his statement right then. The Cocaine was working its way through my system; however, later on that day when I encountered him again, I asked him what he meant by that statement.

He said, "Let me show you the best way to do coke." That was the first time I injected cocaine in my vein, but it wouldn't be the last. What a fucking rush! It launched me someplace that I had never been before. Sweat was falling off my forehead like rain drops and my conversation was going 100 miles per hour. I was in another zone. It was from that day that I was convinced that I had found the ultimate high and from that point on cocaine was the drug for me.

I was shooting cocaine in my veins just about every day and I was going through my money faster than I should, hundreds of dollars with every use. Trying to hold on to the lifestyle that I had built around myself was getting complicated. Things were slipping and there was too much of a demand and the cash wasn't there. I started making mistakes in my eyes and hand coordination and my hustling game was falling off. I was missing important money opportunities. It finally came to an end when a stupid miscalculated mistake caused the life that I had been living to come to a halt.

I got up that morning, took a shower, got dressed and told Gail to handle things for me until I got back. I headed out in my rented car in the direction of 34th Street into the downtown area of St. Petersburg. I parked the car and walked around looking for a good hustle. I went past this jewelry store and from the outside through the window I could see that the place was very busy. I had been here before today was the opportunity I had been waiting for.

I walked in and made my way to the far side of the place. I waited for someone to ask me if I needed any help but none of the workers came over to where I was. I knew that I had entered without notice. Someone had left the counter door unlocked so I took advantage of it. I saw what I wanted and keeping a watch for any sign of being seen. I reached over behind the counter, opened the jewelry case, reached in and snatched a case that held sixteen very expensive looking rings. I closed the case and walked out undetected.

I wasn't finished. I drove to Central Square to a mall. I wanted to do another hustle. If I was going to support my lifestyle, and a demanding cocaine habit I had to make no less than $5,000. I parked the car in the parking lot perhaps too far from where I should have parked it, but I wasn't on my game like I should have been. I left all the rings in the car glove compartment and walked maybe twenty-five to thirty feet to the jewelry shop I had in mind. I had stolen several items and old coins from this shop before.

The owner was a guy in his late senior years he maned the shop by himself, so this was going to be easy and quick. I entered the shop, made small talk with him then began looking around as if I was trying to decide on something to buy. This is where I slipped at not taking the time to check out the possibility that maybe he was watching me.

It was a setup. The display case was unlocked so I reached over slid the door of the display case open, and just gangster Bogart took a case of coins. The owner came from around the counter yelling at me, "what the hell do you think you're doing?" He tried to stop me at the door, but I just pushed past him and exited the shop. He was in pursuit of me hollering, "HEY YOU COME BACK HERE SECURITY!!!!! I tried to lose him, but his loudness attracted the attention of a security guard as well as other people. I was being chased and I knew that the police were on their way. Like a fool I ran over to my rented car. I tried to get my key into the door, but the security guard was doing all that he could to stop me. We are now in a struggle, and it was getting crazy, but I was able to get loose from his grip and I ran in the opposite direction.

I had to hide. I found a good place to do that and waited for quite some time. When I came out of hiding, I didn't see anyone. I walked straight to my car there were no other cars parked around my car damn, it was a setup. I walked over to my car, put my key in the door and the police jumped out hollering," freeze stop!" But I didn't. I jumped in the car, started it and sped away like a mad man out of hell almost running over whoever was in my way. I got out of that parking lot and was gone.

I had to come up with a plan. I parked the car in the parking lot of the hotel. I went up to my room and Gail was still in the room. When I went in, I gave her the all the rings and coins, then called the car rental place made up this story about how I looked out the window and noticed that the car was gone. The guy on the other end of the phone asked me to come down to the rental place to fill out some paperwork.

Now this is where I got stupid. I waited thirty minutes, called back and told him that I came outside and noticed that the car was in the parking lot but not in the area that I had parked it. He still requested that I bring the rental car back to the shop so he can give it a check over and that he would replace the car with another car.

Stupid me I drove to the rental place. I pulled into the parking lot and when I get out of the car the police come out with guns drawn one grabbed me and we struggled, me trying to get my freedom, but it was no use. It was over and everything had caved in that day the lifestyle I was living was over. I sat in county jail for four months before I went to court.

They offered me a sweet deal, one year in the country. I took it with four months already. In all I had to do was no more than six more months in the Clearwater County jail. They offered me a sweet deal, one year in the country. I took it with four months already. In all I had to do was no more than six more months in the Clearwater County jail.

I was happy when my sentence was over. The time in jail gave me the opportunity to think and get my mind and physical ability back on point. Upon my release from jail as I was waiting in the booking/release area waiting to sign my release paper something caught my eye and my mind attention. I noticed a drawer and I can see that there was a good amount of money in it. No one was really minding it.

The two jailers that were on duty were busy doing whatever. I watched and waited for the right opportunity to present itself and when it did like an unseen vision with lightning speed, I went behind the booking counter. The drawer was already open. There were two slots for each denomination of bills. I grabbed enough twenty-dollar bills from each slot, but only enough so it won't be obvious to the eyes. No one saw me and I returned back to where I had been waiting.

I made a call my brother Van and explained to him that it was important for him to come and pick me up as fast as possible. I was given my property and I signed out and waited outside for my brother. He finally arrived and I jumped in his car and told him, "Let's roll." I couldn't wait to get away from there. I told him about what I did, and he laughed and said, "If you have the nerve bro, but you've always been good at what you do."

I bought a good amount of weed with some of the money. During my stay in county jail the people that my brother Van had been working for had run into trouble and the empire that he was working for had taken a fall. My brother made a change in his life. He had a child to take care of, so he was doing the father daddy thing, but true to the game he was a player. I respected his decision.

The money that I had left after buying weed wasn't going to last forever, I had to come up with a way to make money. So, when my brother offered me a job where he was working, I accepted it. I was working at the Orange Blossom Cafeteria and living at my brother's house along with his wife and baby daughter.

# A JOB

My brother Van was working at the Orange Blossom Cafeteria in downtown St. Petersburg. So, it was easy to land me a job. I started out as a dish washer, but in a few months, I went from washing dishes to setting up and arranging the food for the cafeteria buffet line. After the promotion it was easy, I continued working my way up through positions.

Also, from the advice of my brother after he became the cafeteria executive manager. when he needed something prepared, he would tell me, I in turn would assign the task to one of the kitchen workers. That's right I was managing the back of the kitchen. My ability to take charge caught the attention of one of the owner's sons. So not only was I running the back kitchen, but I was also running the catering service for the restaurant as well. That meant being trusted with picking up money from those events.

One of the best things that came from working there was meeting Nancy. She was a white woman several years older than I was. She had sandy brown hair down to her shoulders a very beautiful smile with eyes to match. She always seemed to have a lovely scent, her figure was nice and sexy in every aspect she was attractive. It was my mission to get between her legs, but most of all get from her whatever else I could get. Especially after knowing that her ex who she was still friends with sold large amounts of weed. So, the game began I did my very best to impress her with my style of coolness. often complimenting her in every way that I could.

I filled her head with all kinds of promises and dreams. During working hours when I saw her and the opportunity presented itself, I would often give her the Charmin test (squeeze her on the butt). It was always followed by a slick remark "ooh so soft and squeezable" it that always made her smile.

Often after work we would go out to the parking lot sit in her car listening to disco music over the radio smoke a couple of joints and talk. There were several moments in the car we did more than converse with words. We did some smooching kissing and touching just a few steps from having sex. This particular day was like any other Friday day at work. I was putting some food out on the line when Nancy approached me, asking me if I wanted to go out with her to the Executive Lounge. Of course, I said, but you're going to have to pick me up. I asked her if she knew where Bartlett Park was? She was familiar so the date was planned.

After work I went to the bank cashed my check then head home. After taking a shower I deodorized, splashed on some cologne, and got dressed. Bell bottom pants with a funky shirt. Always the latest gear this was the seventies can ya digg it. I stepped outside the air was nice and cool, but still warm I walked to the park to wait for Nancy.

Five minutes later she arrived I got in the front seat then we rode off. We talked and smoked a joint that put me in a good mood. Her Car the Mark Five it was an amazing site. She parked the car we went inside the music was great. We sat at the bar ordered a drink, I was already high, so the drink just boosted the feeling. Our conversation was just small talk but after a few more drinks she was ready to dance.

I accommodated her to the dance floor. We danced it was the same cycle all throughout the night drinking, dancing, talking and partying the night away. I was as being as cool as can be while Nancy had a few more drinks. By the end of the night, she was very high she made no qualms about her intentions. The club was about to close for the night the next move was on her.

She suggested that we get a room, we didn't have to go anywhere as the hotel was part of the building. As we made our way out the club, I put my arm around her as we walked out the club. The air outside was cool which in turn brought me back to attention. I waited for Nancy as she went inside the hotel lobby to pay for a room.

When she returned, we had to locate the door to match the number on the key to the room. Which wasn't as easy as it sounds, that's how we knew we were fuck up. It was small but sufficient enough to accommodate what we were about to do. We wasted no time with formality. Nancy sat on the bed and began undressing. I watched as she undressed, and I followed her lead. Naked on top of the sheets we began kissing. I was high from the alcohol and drinks and let the moment take over. I felt the warmth of her body and sweetness of her nipples on her breasts, the pleasure aroused my manhood, and my dick was hard and ready.

As I entered into her I felt the warmth and wetness of her pink pussy. She moaned with pleasure as I went further and further in exploring every part of her pussy. I could feel her hands exploring the back of my body and I fucked her putting her in all kinds of positions. She returned the rhythm of my moves. She was at her max and it was proved when she began coming. I was at my max and busted my nut deep in her. I laid on the bed and she lay on my chest while we fell asleep.

The next morning, I awakened Nancy with another round of fucking then we went to take a shower together. Nancy returned the key, then we drove to a restaurant to have breakfast. Afterwards she dropped me off at the park, it wasn't until the following Monday that I would see Nancy again. By then I had told my brother about our encounter. He in turn told his partner so it was no secret within the group.

The look in Nancy eyes the way she acted around me concurred, plus she constantly reminded me of Friday night. The fact was so obvious that she couldn't wait until the next time she could see me. I was young she was just a piece of ass, but as for her it meant more than that. The wolf in me, knowing that I was balls deep in her feelings if I needed something she would buy it for me no hesitation. If I asked her for money, she was pulling out like it was nothing not even a blink.

Knowing that her ex was a weed dealer, I had Nancy bringing me large amounts of weed. All I had to do was to give her a good hard dick fucking or compliment her style when we were out into the night life. We match well together she felt like a star when she was with me. I worked at that restaurant close to a year using and playing Nancy every so often, but the wolf in me missed the hustling game. So, I returned back to hustling on the side.

With working and hustling I now had two sources of incomes. With those two incomes I was able to move out of my brother's apartment and rent a one-bedroom cottage in the Rosa Park neighborhood. I saved up enough money to be able to pay cash for a used Buick Wildcat as well. The top was white, and the bottom half was gold. It was a clean vehicle inside and out, but it was plain in comparison to the standards of the ways cars were jazzed up in the hood.

It took me a few months to get my car the way that I wanted it. But of course, I did. I had the car repainted leaving the top white but the bottom I had re-painted to gold and mixed into the paint gold some silver sparkles. I put all-around two-inch gangster whitewall tires. On the inside I had installed an eight-track tape player, with high quality stereo speakers in the back on both sides of the car doors. On the center of the hood was a silver flying lady.

My house became the meeting point for family and associates and their ladies, my brother Van being who he was dubbed the place HEADQUARTERs.

The place was cool. It had all the necessities of the 70's as it reflected the personalities of all that entered. There was a stereo record player with four extra speakers attached. Two in the living room, and two ran in the bedroom. A black light to reflect the luminous off the black light posters that hung on the walls, spinning psychedelic lights in the corners casting a ray of colors throughout the living room. Along with that were curtain beads hanging from ever doorway with a dark green fish net that was pinned to the four corners of the living room ceiling.

The kitchen refrigerator was always stocked with cold beer, and wine coolers for the visiting ladies if they preferred. I also always had the top of the shelf weed like Sinsemilla gold, or red bud. It wasn't mandatory but if you were one of the chosen members that enjoyed and partook in the availabilities then there was a certain expectation to contribute, preferably money.

# AKRON'S JEWLERYS

I devoted my time to hustling, no more working. I awoke from sleep as I had become accustomed to early in the AM around seven, showered, dressed in the manner that was conducive for my hustling – slacks, dress shirt and a tie. My shoes were Hush Puppies. That was my attire. I didn't drive as walking would be easier if I needed to get away. It was easier to run and hide than to try and drive away.

By the time I got downtown it was no later than eight o'clock. I began looking around for that opportunity that usually comes with the early morning slide. I felt it a 6th sense if you will my wolf sense, something like hustler's intuitions. It kicked in as I passed by an antiquity gold and coin dealer. I knew the sense was usually right. I entered the shop no bell sounded. Behind the counter there seemed to be just one person working, she was busy with an early morning customer, perfect.

I did my best not to draw attention to myself. So far, so good. In every store there's a place that if you knew where to go it will make you unnoticeable, Stealthy I continued slowly, but with caution making my way around looking for the reason why it was this shop had called to me. Then I noticed it. The worker probably unintentional had left the lock off the counter behind the display case. Leaving the counter case unlocked.

Still in Alpha mode with ease and confidence, I quickly made my way over to the unlocked display case. Along the way I made a quick observation of the contents and layout of the items within the display case. All in one motion with a quick glance around to see the position of the customer, and the worker I did my thing.

It was automatic like breathing. I reached over the counter, into the display case having already a mental picture of what and where items were at, I grabbed in accordance with what I remembered; a case of assorted rings. Quickly I put it into my front pants pocket. With another quick look at my surroundings coast was still clear. So, I took a plastic coin holder. That was enough. I was never a greedy hustler.

I slid the door of the display case closed just in case so as to not to draw attention. Now for my exit. I just walked out of the store door. Then I went into one of the many other stores in the downtown area and walked around eye shopping until I felt comfortable enough to leave.

I walked to my usual fence but the store wasn't open so I decided to go see if I could make a deal with this black guy that I had heard had opened and owned a jewelry store. I had hoped that this would be a good business opportunity for him and me. As well as make a new connection. You know help get his business up with quality jewelry at a reasonable price ya dig.

I knew this would be my first dealing with him and I was taking serious chance but taking a chance in this line of work is part of what it's about. I went home to get my car as I had to drive to the north side of town to where his business was. I pulled into the parking lot and parked. With just the rings in my possession I entered. The sound of a bell gave a warning that I had entered the store and a business dressed black guy close to the age of forty came from the back of the store to the front and introduced himself. His name was Mr. Akrons.

My intention was to try and get to know something about him and for me to get a feel for his personality. After exchanging pleasantries and talking shop for a while it was time for me to tell him the real reason for me being here.

"I have some quality and expensive diamond rigs for sale," I said to him.

"Would you be interested in buying them?"

"Show me what you have," he said.

I showed him ten of the best assorted rings and he said that he needed to take them in the back of the shop so that he could check them and determine their value. Even though there were price tags on each ring. I knew that they were just the asking prices and not the actual value of each ring. So, I was alright with him doing so.

As I waited for him to do whatever it was, he had to do, I took the time to view through the glass display case all the items that he had on display. When he returned, he informed me that he was not interested in doing business with me. It was after he returned less than what I had given him was when the shit really hit the fan. Instead of handing me ten rings, as I know I had given him. This silly muthafucka handed me only five rings. I told him that I gave him ten rings and not five, but he is trying to convince me that I was wrong. This head-butting contest was not getting anywhere, so before he would decide to threaten me with calling the police. I humbly accepted his bull shit and took the five rings back.

All the while I am thinking I cannot let this guy get away with ripping me off. You are not about to outshine the master. I knew that I had to do something. My mind recalled not seeing any locks on the display case in his store, I went into Wolf mode formulated a quick plan. I made my way to the door as if I were leaving. But I was not actually leaving. I pulled open the door, made the motion as if I were stepping out, but made a quick turnaround to see what he was doing.

He was enthralled with what he had done, he failed to take warning of the situation for himself to be certain of my moves. It was time for me to show him the consequence of his actions. I made a quiet but quick beeline back into the store. Like a wolf in the wind, I went behind the counter, positioned behind the display case quick but silently, staying low out of view with my Alpha scenes on top alert. I slide open the doors to every display case. I took just about every piece of jewelry he had on display in that muthafucka. All while he drooled over the punk ass five rings.

On my way out behind me was the sound of the door alarm Bing! I hid within the area of the building and peeked out from where I was hiding and watched as Mr. Akron looked around in search of me. I felt justified in what I had done. After all it was his own doing that initiated the game, we just played. Once he went back into his shop I got in my car and drove away back to my place. A little way back, I had heard about this shop that dealt in boosted items. I had not done business there before, but after all that. I did not want to be in procession of all this jewelry either. I needed to get rid of all of it as quickly as possible now.

I drove home parked my car then went inside and changed my clothing. I put everything in a velvet pouch. I then left my place this time I headed out on foot to uptown St. Petersburg, the shop was on Ninth Street. Mr. Atkins had already put the word on the grape vine amongst the fellow jewelers to be on the lookout for me. So, when I walked into the shop fifteen minutes later the owner already knew who I was and what had transpired.

Skipping the formalities, I went right to business. "Excuse me" I said. "I heard that you're the person to see". "What do you have"? He asked, "I have some jewelry that I want to sell but I don't have no identification", I replied. "No problem", he said, "let me have a look at what you have" he asked me. I handed him a sufficient amount of jewelry, but not all of what I had. He looked at the items then said that he was interested in buying what I had, but he was on the phone taking care of some important business and needed a few minutes to finish. That if I do not mind waiting until he took care of the call, then him and I could conclude our business.

Cool, I said and waited. He went to the back of his shop, I waited with no idea that he was calling Mr. Akron to inform him that I was at his store. It had to be ten maybe fifteen minutes later when the owner returned and handed me the items that I had given him back, I was almost leery. I felt something was not right by the way he kept looking at me. Then at the front door it was my hustler's intuition.

My Wolf sense was going crazy it was intuition right too. As I was putting all the jewelry in a velvet pouch, I looked up out the window of the shop, and noticed a green Buick Rivera slow down and parked a few feet away from the shop. I recall seeing that car parked in the parking lot in front of the building of Akron jewelry.

The driver side car door opened, and Mr. Akron stepped out, he for sure did not have a smile on his face either. He was accompanied by two six foot, two hundred plus pound looking muthafuckas. I could tell from his demeanor, and appearance that he was not there to play checkers either. I had to make quick decisions. I looked left, then right. The shop had two sides; each side had independent entrances giving me the options of exiting either side.

I looked back around by this time the chicken shit owner had cowardly gone to the back of the shop leaving me there by myself. Not wanting to get caught with the goods in hand, I had to hide the velvet pouch I noticed on the shelf in the store was an assortment of jewelry boxes. I put the velvet pouch in one of the jewelry boxes, then I made my exit by going to the opposite side of the store. In the opposite direction from where I saw Mr. Akron and his partners entering.

I could tell that the big guy had a pistol in his waist. He started reaching for it, as they entered the store. I exited stage left out the other side, running as fast as I could, to avoid my pursuers. Booking it I hit patterns up and down streets, down back alleys, cutting across avenues, bending corners making sure to lose those jive ass turkeys. I could hear tires spinning out in the distance. I knew it had to be Akron's Buick in hot pursuit trying to find out which way I had went. But trying to run down a wolf in his own forest is like trying to bottle lighting good luck with that!

I cut through the back-alley ways, and across yard until I finally made it back to my place. I quickly went inside to wait, and quietly gather my thoughts. All the while listening, while peeking out my hotel window until I felt comfortable that I had lost my pursuers. It was a long night waiting, contemplating, knowing that I had to get back to the shop! There was no way I was not retrieving the velvet pouch that I had hidden in one of the jewelry boxes.

I did not get much sleep that night. I spent my time getting high with girls and drinking. However in-between I did manage to formulate plan that would go perfectly with the situation. I woke up to the sound of the early morning birds singing their wake-up songs. Outside the hotel window I saw the light of day had broken through the nights haze. The Florida morning sun graced the sky. I dressed in all dark clothing and told my girls that I will be back.

I floated down the stairs, and out the door into the cool warm Florida air. I walked up 34th street, then on down to 9th street to my destination. When I got there, I sat on the bench at the bus stop that was across from the business. Waiting for the owner to arrive. After waiting for what seemed like eternity the owner finally arrived. I waited to watch him park. Then when he went to the front of the store to unlock the shop. I quickly sprang like a wolf into action across the street. By the time he realizes what was going on. I had bow-guarded my way pass him into the shop. He walked in behind me automatically he knew who I was. I went straight to the jewelry box open it up and retrieved the velvet pouch of jewelry. I knew that I did not have much time, because I saw the owner was on the phone. I knew he had to be calling the police.

It was early in the morning; the police station was only a few blocks away too. With package in hand, I was out the door and began running. I could hear the sirens of police cars in hot pursuit of me. I understood that I did not have that much of a head start, so I made a wolfs decision. I ran into a field that was overgrown with grassy bushes, and trees. A perfect hideaway for what came next. I decided the best thing for me to do was to bury the pouch somewhere that I would remember. So that if I did get caught by the police, I would deny any knowledge of what they are talking about. My thinking was that would be good enough and the police would have to let me go.

# Lady Buns

Brookline was a small town so remembering its streets and getting around was no problem. I got another job working at a car wash in Brookline just a few minutes away from the Brookline center. That was where I first saw Ronda.

My fellow workers and I would often get together to go for lunch at some of the local sandwich shops in the area. There we were walking, talking about some of the inner cities where we all had lived like Roxbury, Dorchester, Mattapan, and Jamaica Plain. I was glad to hear that these communities consisted of not only African Americans, but also Spanish folks those are my peoples.

They also talked about the different clubs, and the nightlife that goes on within the area. Now this was exactly the part and of the city life that I was looking for. On this afternoon as the fellas and I are headed to get lunch we walked pass one of the local pharmacies in downtown Brookline.

There in the window of the store working behind the counter was this tall fine coco brown big booty fine ass female. Her hair was in long braids, with beads on the end of every bread. She wore a pair of dark gray jogging pants her booty was bouncing like Jell-O with every effort she made.

Damn! I said in a somewhat upper tone look at that ass. The guys said that they all had noticed her for some time, but no one had the nerve to go into the store to talk to her. I was still a little hesitant about talking to what looked to be a city girl. But one day as the fellas and I walked pass the store, as I was looking at her then our eyes caught each other's! she waved at me I smiled back she had a beautiful smile with full lips but that was that.

But as faith would have it another day as I was heading to work, me still being a little country decided to hitch hike. A white 1968 Jet Star Oldsmobile pulls over, stops. When I get in the car it was the lady from the store. I admired the way she kept her car clean inside, and out. The interior of the car was red. I thanked her an told her where I was headed.

I was surprised by her boldness when she produced a joint and lit it up. The music she was listening to was jazz. I asked her name it was Ronda. Months later I would nickname her "Lady Buns". We talked just about the whole time! I felt we were hitting it off, I wanted to introduce myself properly, but just could not build up the nerve. So, I ask her "where do you live at"? She said "Roxbury". She told me one time she was in the Air force. I said," I would like to hear more about that", she smiled. We had reached my destination. As I was getting out the car before she could drive off, I asked her if it was possible for us to get together this afternoon for lunch. She said yes, then we made a time to meet for lunch.

The fellas at work asked me who was that! I told them who it was, and that I am having lunch with her. They did not want to believe it. But when lunch came there, she was standing waiting in front of the store. I walk up smoother then a muthafucka to her and said "hello", then introduce her to my coworkers. She said, hello to them as they all stared in disbelief. With a wolfish grin I chucked up the peace sign, told them that I'll see them back at the car wash after I have lunch with her, then we bounced.

We went to her favorite Chinese restaurant. I told her that I knew nothing know about ordering Chinese food. So, Rhonda ordered tea and lunch for us. Our conversation was more about her, but when she told me that she lived in Roxbury I got excited. I wanted to know more, I had heard about the lifestyle, and the nightlife in Roxbury that was where I needed to go.

After lunch before we went back to our jobs. I asked her for her telephone number, when she gave it to me my fellow workers gave me praises. I thought about her the rest of the day and could not wait to get home to call her. I dialed area code 617 followed by her phone number a female answered the phone and I asked to speak to Rhonda, the voice asked me to wait while she goes to get her. A few minutes later Rhonda's lovely voice came thought the phone we talked for a while, throughout our conversation I found her to be a remarkably interesting conversationalist. At the coming end of our conversation, I asked her if she would be interested in going out with me?

She said "yes".

So, we made plans to go out that coming Friday night, which was one day away. I was extremely excited, as I made my plans to hit the city, with a cool city lady. I made mention to her that I was not too familiar with Boston. She said that she could pick me up at my grandmothers' apartment after giving her the address we disconnected.

Later that day I told my grandmother about Rhonda, as well as our plans for Friday. when I told her where Rhonda lived, my grandmother was not all that thrilled to hear it. Not only was I talking to her but had made plans with a woman from Roxbury. Roxbury was considered the ghetto with a not so pleasant reputation. I dismissed my grandmother's view and pressured my own.

I was looking for a female companion, and Rhonda was beautiful and sexy. I thought about her throughout the night and was overly excited when Friday arrived. When I called Rhonda so that we could coordinate, to my dismay for some reason she had to cancel our night together. I did not bother to ask her for a reason, I was not tripping Friday for me was just another day.

The following week on Monday, she and I were able to meet up during her lunch break. She explained to me what happen, I understood. For me it was just one day, I was not about to give up on this new relationship. That just gave me future reservation for other times. I went back to what I had to do hustling making that money living in the city.

Brookline Massachusetts became the first town in which I would reinvent my hustling game. Brookline was one of those upscale New England towns not inundated with crime. Most of its occupants drove luxury cars and lived in moderately lavish homes. Its business part of the town was not use to my slicker than quick activities, so I took advantage of the anonymity.

I operated with easy it was like taking candy from a baby. I would slip unnoticed into the back of stores, and office buildings to locate the safe. Often the safe would be unlocked, good for the pilfering of stacks of money. I even came quit often upon money bags on top of desks in manager's offices. I always made sure those bags made it to the bank. Never the obvious, to ensure that a wolf remained unnoticed.

I learned the most vulnerable times, that were the best time for hustling at least for me was in the earlier morning. Before anyone had their coffees, while they were still discombobulated not fully aware. I was making money hand over fist. So, I had to decide hustle, or go to work? Easy choice right! Hustling of course, there was no other choice remember I was committed to the game. With every hustler that I did, I knew that I would have to expand my ground by venturing further away from Brookline, getting inevitably closer into the big city of Boston, with all its swiftness. This venture would be an opportunity for me to acclimate myself with the ins and outs of the streets of Boston.

Later, I would return back to the location that I had marked in my mind to retrieve my bounty. I looked and decided on a location memorably. I picked up a plastic bag from of the ground put the velvet pouch of jewelry put it in the plastic bag. With my hands I dug a hole in the ground as far as I could. Then buried the bag of jewelry like a pirate's treasures. I then continued with my get away run, trying to get back to my house, then I heard a helicopter! Damn I thought! I tried but my efforts were fruitless. They finally captured me I was arrested; my run had finally come to an end.

My alibi did not work as well as I thought it would. So, I had to spend months in Clearwater County jail. Thing about my case is, I thought I was going to beat this criminal case this time. However, when the public defender informed me. That the state was bringing in, not only the guy I stole the jewelry from. But also, the guy from the store that I attempted to sell the jewelry to. As a witness for the state, to testified against me. I knew my position in the situation had changed. So, I took the deal that the state was offering two years in prison. It was after doing that sentence that I would have to leave St. Petersburg, FL and move to Boston.

# THE JEWELS of THE CITY

There was no direction for me, I usually just let my primal instinct direct me to the hustle. This other morning it leads me to this jewelry building downtown, The Jewel of The City. I enter the jewelers building which was a wholesale retail distribution operation. I went from floor, to floor up and down the hallway from every angle, nothing but jewelry store, after jewelry store. Gold, silver, platinum jewels of all kinds. Rubies, sapphires, semi and precious stones, Diamonds everywhere sparkling in their brilliance of fiery morning light. I was hypnotized, spellbound, captivated in the euphoria. I knew at that moment that I was back in an element I was familiar with, so many money possibilities.

I was already familiar, overly educated with the knowledge of these items from those pass years of hustling with such rarities in Florida. I believed that knowledge would enable me to pass through like a Jedi master using mind trick techniques in any of these numerous jewelry stores, throughout this building. First thing was first thought. I knew for me to get a better understanding of what I was facing. I would have to make several visits into this building to get used to the layout, as well as the people's movements. Like a wolf scouting the forest I was at that building at least twice a week so I would start to blend in.

It was like a personal quest, to learn all I can about the ins and outs of the treasure filled building. The first thing I had to do was establish a good repour amongst the people working within the place. I had to perform without flaws. The role was a young man dealing in and try to make my way around the jewelry business.

I went to that building twice a week going from floor to floor, visiting two or more stores. Where I would have a business conversation with different salespersons, and gemologist. All the while learning and comprehending the jeweler's lingo, developing a comfort within the realm in which as was in. Getting familiar with the surrounding, and functions of some of the shops, in order to determine which stores offed the opportunity that I was looking for.

It took me less than a month to get to hustling. I had always respected that appearance was especially important when hustling around the big city and in the line of business I was about to embark on. Having already snatched up serval expensive suits, dress shirts, and shoes, from Lords and Taylor, and Filenes which were two of many of Boston high expensive stores. I was ahead of to the game. Boston at that time always seem to me like it was fall season. I was up and downtown early in morning doing my best to make money, but so far it seemed like things were not working to my benefit.

It was some time past noon, so I decided to take on the challenge of the jewelry building. There was a security guard seated at a front desk, but I walked right past him, bided him a good afternoon. Then proceeded like I work there or was on a business quest. I took the stairs instead of the elevator. I step out of the stairways onto one of the floors, then went to hustling. Going in and out of serval stores without success.

I continued hustling, then I got that wolfish 6th sense I entered. There were eight, maybe fifteen customers in the place. I did my best to not draw attention to myself doing my best to be unnoticed, blending into what I considered the blind. I walked around the store looking for the opportunity that called to me, then I saw it there it was a black box setting on one of the shelve behind the counter, I knew exactly what it was a ring box!

Like an Alpha in the wild I could precisely pinpoint its distant, will within a slight of eye arm reach. I gave one last look at my surrounding, no one within the place was paying attention to me. I knew that I had to take the chance it was now or never.

Like smooth but slick I casually made my way over to the area where the box was. I knew the exact magician like motion swapping the black box in one quick look. I reached over the front display case grabbed the black box from its location, tucked it down the front of my pants buttoned up my coat, while breathing a sigh of relief all in one stroke. There was no hesitation, no one said anything I had gotten away with it, just as quickly I left.

I did not yet know of a fence to sell these items to, but I knew that just like my hustling years in Florida all I had to do was search. Subsequently I knew I could find someone within the same building. In due time I would for sure find someone that had some larceny in their heart. This was a cutthroat industry. There were sixteen beautiful diamond rings in that case. I asked $700 for each ring but settled for $500 for each ring. I got $8,000 no questions, no explanation. I gave my grandparents $2,500. Then I went to enjoy the surrounding of the city and its night life.

I had to take some time out of the game to just live, you know enjoy the fruits of my work. It would months later before I was back in the game. The jewelry building became one of my top hustling places. It turned out to be one very profitable hustling adventure for me. I had now become more familiar with the terrain, and bus system. I was becoming more, and more a part of the city. Adapting to all its smells, its constant flow of peoples, merchants, and of course the commence.

As I moved around those buildings, and streets, I was always on the lookout for an opportunistic hustle. Day in and day out, I was on my grizzly. Hustling through the bustle, up and down the city of Boston going from store to store. Inquiring, looking, asking questions, and learning what it was that I had to do to achieve that necessary opportunity. It was my continuous efforts that allowed me to happen upon this one store. In there they used the practice of replacing the space of rings they sold with a ring size round plastic chip.

I knew what I had to do, I knew the city now too, so I knew exactly where to go get those same plastic chips. I took them instead of buying them it is the way u leave no way to trace it back. If I knew where they were sold, anyone could come trace back receipts. I went back home after snatching them up to set plans for the next morning. The next day, I got up, got dressed and ready to go gather the chips. I headed out the door making my way to the train station, to catch the rail downtown. I got off the subway then headed Up from the belly of the station, into the city heading straight towards the jewelry building.

I made my way up the stairs to the store that replaced the sold rings with a plastic chip. The store was open and busy. Once inside it was time for me to go into straight Alpha mode. Now I am looking around for the right mark. Then I saw it! She was a middle-aged employee unoccupied and waiting. She was sizing me up too from where she was posted. As I was looking at her right on point, she asked me if I needed some help, it was time to work my plan.

" Yes, I said to her. I'm interested in purchasing a diamond ring for my fiancée."

She asked me how much I was planning on spending.

"$2500" I said, "but if it goes over a little that's alright".

She retrieved one of the many cases of diamond rings from out of the display case. Places it on top of the counter between the two of us. She removed one of the diamond rings, showed it to me then I listened, as she did her sales pitch. After it was time for me to impress her with my knowledge of diamonds, as well as gold. This ploy was to take away any thought of uneasiness, get her to relax so that I could do my thing without misconception.

I went into the four c's, telling her the real price in comparison to what was being asked for the ring. Not being satisfied I asked to see another ring. She showed me another, at the same time I asked if she had a jewelry loop. I peered at the diamond through the loop while asking her, what she thought of its qualities. In between our conversation, I noticed that she had taken her attention off the case of diamond rings in front. Still discussing the ring, I took the opportunity to take advantage. As smooth as slick, I took two rings replacing the vacancy with two plastic chips all the while drawing her attention away from what I was doing. The magician's sleight of hand. It was time to make my exit. I told the sales lady that I like the price, but I wanted to check with a few more stores in the building before I make my final decision. After leaving, I go immediately to my fence in the same building. The diamond rings sold no problem $1500 easy.

I was still living with my grandparents but by this point in my life Rhonda and I were seeing one another on a regular basis. I knew having her come over to where I was living was out of the equation. But we continued seeing each other mostly on her terms, being that she had a car. I had to rely on her to pick me up for either dinner, or just to see each other get high and talk. The night would end with an occasional smooching the relationship had not yet become physical. At the same time, I did manage to meet one of the many Spanish ladies that I noticed in the neighborhood. She was walking back to her apartment from the store. This acquaintance would prove to be more of a convenience, being that she only lived a few blocks from where I was living with my grandparents.

If you remember there was a store that I was going in by climbing up the wall in the back alley. I went back there months later to make another hustle since it was still profitable resource. This time I grabbed bigger luggage bags from inside the store. I climbed inside the small space, up the ladder, then out into the men's department. With the extra-large size duffle bag in hand, I took Calvin Klein jeans, IZOD, and Polo style shirts. Climbed back in and went to the lady's department grabbed up some fashionable Jordache jeans.

I exited down the escalator duffle bag in hand packed with clothing. Always keeping in mind my people love wearing the latest fashions.  I had to go into the hood for this hustle, the only person that I knew at that time was Rhonda (Lady Bunz). She had no idea that I was a hustler, but tonight it was time to introduce her to the other side of me. Shed some light into my world, and exactly what I do. We made a date to meet around 6 p m on Friday, which was a plus because most people get paid at the end of the week.

Tonight, was special I was dressed to impress. I heard a car horn, looked out the window it was her. I picked up the duffle bag full of clothing said goodbye to both grandparents then headed out the door. I put the duffle bag in the back seat of the car, got up front and kissed her hello. As we were on our way to Dudley in Roxbury, she asks me

"What was in the big ass bag, are we going to do laundry? I told her "No its not laundry". "This new clothing". She asked me," clothing for what"?

That was when I told her my plan hoping that she would help me. I told her that I will show her what I have when she parks.

We arrived at Dudley. I grabbed the duffle bag, opened it up so that she could get a good look at what was inside. After looking at all the items, too much joy, she said that she knew exactly where to go. But first she wanted to know if she could get a couple pair of jeans for herself. The place we went to was called Roscoes' a night club located in Dudley Station down in Roxbury, it was Black owned and operated. When I stepped into the club, I felt what I had been missing, the comfort of being back in the hood amongst my people, the lifestyle that I had come to love being accustomed to.

The club goers were dressed in the fashions of the time, the place was genuinely nice and clean. We sat down. I put the duffle bag in a seat next to me, then the waitress came over. I ordered drinks for myself and Lady Bunz. The music was right on they were jamming like a muthafucka. I felt the beat, the soulful sound of the Rhythm and Blues being spun by the Disc Jockey DJ Hellafied. This was the time for me to blend and understand the people. After all I was in their territory it was a new environment of the city for me.

The drinks finally arrived, with my drink in hand I told Rhonda that I was going to make my way around the club to get acclimated with the people. You know a wolf it was like I had a master's in communication. I made my way around the club kicking game like a soccer ball.

Several different folks were interested in what I had to sell. Then I met the owner of the club himself! He was sitting at the back end of the bar enjoying his position. I introduced myself. After conversating about the club, along another things. I mention to him that I had some cool threads for sale. He was digging what I was putting down then asked to see what I had.

Returning with the duffle bag we sat in the corner. As much darkness as possible to take care of business. I had his size in pants and Polo shirts, I made $75 from that first sale. By the time I sat down with Bunz the word had already got around. Cats began asking me for items a couple more sales real quick fast. Rhonda excused herself to the lady's room. When she returned, she informed me that a few of the girls she spoke to wanted jeans. I gave her the required pair of jeans. Shop was open.

When she returned she handed me $150. We sold every damn item of clothing that was in that duffle bag. So, I asked the owner if I could put the duffle bag behind the bar until I leave. It was time to party with my lady with another round of drinks. We danced and partied until the last call for alcohol. Before heading to our destination, we stopped for a late-night snack at Jessie's. The conversation was small talk mixed in with the sound of smooth jazz as she drove the car.

# A RHONDA-FUL NIGHT

It was late in the night when she pulled up to her house. Rhonda led the way, I followed her up the stairs my eyes were glued to her big ass and caught up in the rhythm.

The apartment was not fancy or big, but it was clean warm and comfortable. I sat down at the table pulled out a joint and fired it up. She went into what I could see was the bedroom. There was a curtain that separated the two rooms. I heard the music coming from the bedroom it was tuned to W.I.L.D. Then she returned, she sat at the table with me I passed her the joint she took a few pulls, past it back the music was sounding good the whole time together it helped set the mood. Few words were said as we smoked then things began to happen.

I kissed her, she reciprocated together as we found our way to the world of pleasure as the kissing led to something else. I felt my desire for her raise in my pants a feeling that I had wanted for so long. My hands began to touch her body. I could feel the heat of her desire under her blouse, as her nipples began to erect until there were hard under my touch. I stood up delicately taking her by the hand, she followed me into her bedroom. Everything went into automatic as we found the bed slowly, I removed her blouse unfastening her bra reviling two firm breasts with erected nipples the flame rose inside of her as it was in me. After a moment of foreplay, she undressed so did I we were naked holding one another.

The bed became my canvas as we began to paint our masterpiece, I felt the warmth of her body I looked at her body admiring the chocolate beauty before me. I reached behind her embracing her big ass. Something that I have wanted to do for so long, it was firm but soft my hand began to touch her all over. Kissing her, she responded to my advances. When my hand made its way between her legs, it was warm as I made my way up her thighs to her clit. I felt the desire in the moistness of her pussy, it was hot flowing with sweet candy juice.

I started rubbing her clit with my finger, she began moving to the rhythm of the song of love. Moaning with desire and passion, as I conducted. My desire for her was at an all-time high. I was ready for peak performance in the pussy Olympics. I climbed on top of her she opened her legs to receive my manhood. She moaned as I enter her going deeper and deeper, inch after inch. I was onto her pussy like an artist. She was painting her picture with the motions of every move that she made. I found my way back to her erected nipples tasted the flavor of her sweet body once more. I wetted one of my fingers with spit made my way between her big, beautiful ass. I slowly played around her tight hole inserting a little bit of my finger. As I was fucking her, she let out a moan I could feel her pussy get wetter with ecstasy. I changed the situation slowly made my way down her belly. I was on the passage that led to her honeycomb hide out going to find her secret.

I tasted then licked her pussy until she exploded. I waited as she enjoyed the pleasure of the moment. She lay in my arms for a while until I kissed her, she responded so we went at it once again. Engulf in our passion throughout the night until we both exploded, she laid in my arms as we drifted off to sleep.

I woke up feeling the sunlight of the morning on my face. I lifted the blanket up so that I can admire her beautiful sexy body. The sight of her had reawaken my desire. The cool air stirred her, I kissed her lips, then I climbed back on top of her we made morning love.

She got up went to the bathroom. I heard the shower when she came out, I went in. I then showered, dressed came out of the bathroom to the smell of bacon! There was a plate of bacon, eggs, and grits waiting on the table for us to eat together. We had some small talk after that, until she took me back to my grandparents' apartment. Always a wonderful time with Rhonda.

Money does not last long, when you get it the way I was getting it. Eventually I would have to get back to my grind. It was Saturday I had no reason to go hustling. I plenty of bread in my pocket from last night sales. I called lady bunz to see how she was doing to sweeten up her heart, we talked for a while then I asked her if she had anything planned for tonight. She said she had planned on staying home, but if I wanted to come over to her place, I was more welcomed, and she would cook dinner for me. I asked her what train and or bus do I have to catch she gave me the information. I headed that way around 6.

I thought to myself, how different that was for a lady to ask me over for a home cooked meal. I had become so accustomed to the hustler lifestyle eating on the go. As those in the life that spend most of their time on the streets, living in hotels, and motels. The females usually in my life were ladies of the night not ones that cooked dinner.

But this relationship with Rhonda seems to have something special. Maybe it was in the way she looked, or how she carried herself. But whatever it was I willing to dedicate my time, and effort into understanding what it was. Also, she was the kind of lady that complemented my style. I caught the bus then the train into Dudley station. Then I found a pay phone to called her to tell her where I was. she gave me direction to her house. I went down Dudley Street until I got to Mount Pleasant Street. I never f. when I got to number 22, I knocked.

Rhonda came down to let me in I followed her up the stairs to the second floor. Where I met her mother, sisters, and brother. Everyone went about doing their thing, Rhonda and I went to the kitchen. I sat at the table as she finished cooking dinner. She made chili over white rice it was delicious. But like most black families everyone fixed themselves something ate and went about their way.

Rhonda and I sat at the table to eat. We talked about nothing specific just life in general. She didn't bring up anything about the new clothing that I had on, but she being a lady that lived in the hood she had to have an idea that my threads were fly. After dinner we sat in the living room, watched television, and acted like teenagers. After an hour of what was kissing and touching it was time for me to be getting back to where I lived, I said goodbye to her family as I was leaving. Rhonda dropped me off at the apartment, with a good night kiss she drove away. I completed what was left of my weekend chilling at home listening to records and drinking.

# Connection In The Combat Zone

Monday rolled around it was time to get back into the hustling game. Illegal money never last long especially with my lifestyle. I needed to stay ahead of the game hustling was what I love it was my job.

It was the beginning months of winter in Boston. The air was cold but there was no snow on the ground yet. So, I decided the dress for me today would be the businessman appeal. I sported a charcoal gray Bill Blast suit dress shirt. Along with a rep tie, black Bostonian shoes, and my over coat was brown camel hair.

It had been some time since I hustled out of the jewelers building. So that would be my main destination, as well as any other possibilities that may arise along the way. I hopped aboard, what I believe was the orange line subway. Then made a few stops to change trains headed towards Boston. I exit the bowls of the tunnel onto the city streets. Downtown Boston was now a city that I came to love with its complexities of colossally tall buildings. As well as hundreds of thousands of people wrapped up in their own world, making their way to their daily destination.

I was now one of them, but with a different agenda. I was more familiar with the layout of the city of Boston its building as well most of the in and out of its streets. As wolf this was my new forest, Alphas become acclimated quick. So, getting around was becoming less of a problem.

As I made my way up Washington Street. I was in full Alpha mode, ears and eyes on super sense, for any opportunity on my way. But nothing presented itself. I arrived at my destination, I entered the lobby looking, and feeling in full confidence, as if I belonged there. There was a security guard sitting at the front desk, I casually strolled right pass him, pass the elevator. I Walked up the stairs going up floor, to floor walking around just waiting for it finally kick in that 6th sense, that wolf alarm. Me I knew that there was a good hustle somewhere, I just had to find it. I walked down the corridor admiring the exclusiveness of diamonds, gold, and other precious items dazzling from jewelry store windows.

Then I made my decision from the tug at my hustling scenes. You had to be buzzed into the individual establishments in the building, it always presents a challenge making a mistake was not an option. It meant my freedom being on the top of my game was just as important as breathing today would be a test.

The place had 8 maybe 11 customers already in the shop when I entered. From behind the counter came the words "good morning, sir, how might I assist you". He looked to be in his late forties, but I was on the top of my game my appearance said money. Along with the knowledge of a jeweler. I was as close to being a gemologist as any other professional. I gather up my confidence, went into hustler mood, then I would deploy an old hustler's trick called the diversion game.

"Yes, good morning". I responded, "I'm in the market for an engagement ring". But I want to buy the center diamond separate from the surrounding diamonds. I prefer to choose the design of the ring myself. I knew that this meant viewing the diamond independently not just a diamond ring that was already designed. He asked me how much I was planning on spending. I said somewhere in the neighborhood of $1,500 to $2,500, adding that I would prefer the center stone to be of a round brilliant cut. Then we can decide on selecting the smaller surrounding stones to complement the center stone.

"Excellent" he said.

He politely excused himself, turned around going into the black safe that was directly behind him. When he turned back around, he had a black 8x4 box in his hands. He sat the box down on the counter. Then proceeded to produce a jeweler's cloth. He placed the cloth on the counter between the two of us. He opened the box removed one of the numerous folded fine texture white packages. When he unfolded the package there were 10 to 15 round brilliant cut diamonds. Each one had to for sure be valued within the price range that I said I was willing to spend.

It was time for me to go into Alpha mode, exercise all that I had learned from the many years of being in the game. First thing win his trust. I was dressed to impress, I had that won. Now it was time to captivate him with my skills, flex some knowledge earning his respect all in one motion. He picked up one of the diamonds from the many with a jeweler's tweezer. He used his jewelers' loop to view it, while we talked about its particulars. He mentioned it was a GIA then went right into pitching his sale. when he was almost at the end of his pitch. I ask if I could view the diamond for myself.

"Of course," he responded. He hands me the diamond still clenched in the tweezers. It was game time before he could even pass me his jeweler's loop. I reached into my vest pocket pulled out my gold color jewelers eye attached to a gold chain. I knew from the look on his face that I had captivated him. He was now hooked. I stepped back out of wolf mode then I went into my gemologist mode. As I'm viewing the diamond, I make a false assessment about the rating of the diamond in reference to one of the four c's "clarity". I see more carbon specks, or inclusion then I was hoping for. These imperfections can occur in a diamond since diamonds are derived from coal. I said to him "if I'm going to spend $1500 to $2500, I was expecting a diamond with fewer carbon specks."

I was sending my game at him you could sense it was working. I handed the diamond back so that he had to take a second look to recheck. I knew he would have to close one of his eyes in order to examine the diamond through his jeweler loop. His attention would be focused on the diamond. I knew he was just enough in the blind spot for me to make my move. I knew I only had seconds swift as an alpha on its pray with no pack to assist in the hunt I executed. Magician quick, I reached into the open black box that was on the counter. In one quick smooth motion, without drawing attention to what I was doing, delicately I removed one of the white packages slipping it into my vest pocket.

After he finished viewing the diamond, he said that he did not see the inclusions. So, playing the diversion game like it was Atari. I retrieved the tweezers from him along with the diamond, reviewing for another time so minutes. Then I asked for a cloth to clean my jeweler's eye. Handing me a cloth, I clean my loop to attempt an honest better look. Then apologized for my mistake explaining that it was particles on the glass of my loop.

We looked at a couple more diamonds until we agreed on the price. He places that jewel on the cloth. Then replaced the package in the box, putting everything back in the safe. Afterward we viewed some smaller stones. These were to complement the larger center stone at another $2000.

We discussed serval types of setting that he thought would be best for the diamonds. Excusing himself, he returned with serval individual plastic bags each containing 8 to 10 gold ring setting. As we were discussing the different setting types. I divert his attention away from the plastic box.

When I knew the opportunity was right. I reached into the box grabbed three packages, in my pocket they went. We talked about a few more things, finally we came to a decision about the type of ring that was best set for the diamonds. I acted super interest, so he quoted me a price. I told him that I wanted to do some more shopping around before I make my decision. But as of this moment their price is reasonably likely to win.

Handshakes, thanks and smiles were exchanged. He hands me his business card, writes on the back of the card the price, and the style of the ring that we agreed upon. He pressed the button activating the buzzer to unlock the door. Letting me out, I flashed a Wolfish grin to myself as I made my way down the hallway.

Quickly I make my way down the stairs out the building, into the busy streets of downtown Boston. The sound of the city, filled with thousands of pedestrians, traffic everyway I knew I was good. I had made it pass my first hurdle. My vest pocket had no less than $12k in diamonds. My pants pocket was looking a decent spades hand as well. Another $4k and possible.

Even thought I had been selling jewelry to different dealers. For this, I did not want to deal with any of them located in the jewelers building. I needed to find another fence, one that could handle the type of money that I would be requesting. I do not know why I went in the direction that I did. But I ended up in what was known as The Combat Zone! Upon arriving my attention was drawn to one strip club. Although there was many to choose from at the time. There was one that stood out amongst the rest. It was called the Intermission and it was wide open.

I went inside, but before I could look around for someone I was confronted at the door by this big Italian man. He had to be a bouncer. He asked me "what did I want"? I could tell from the look of things that the club was not exactly open to everyone. I came straight to the point. I told him that I had some business involving diamonds, that I would like to speak to the proprietor of this establishment to ask if they were interested in buying. He asked me to "wait at the door". I watched as he went over to a table to talk to this guy that was sitting there going over some papers.

The big guy returned escorted me to where the man was seated, I was told to "hold on". After gathering his paperwork up, he invited me over to sit down. His name was Tony he was an Italian gentleman with prefixed ideas that fit every part of the Mob stereotype. To this I concluded that there was no need for me to beat around the muthafuckn bush with him.

I kept it a buck introducing myself as the Wolf, extending my hand as I sat down. Getting straight to the point of business. "I have some quality expensive diamonds for sale". "Are you interested in buying them"? He looked at me in a serious way, rubbing his hands together. Then with a thick Italian accent said.

"Aye Let me see what you got"?

I pulled out one of the packages opened it showed him the diamonds. Shit caught his attention stupid quick. He shrugged that we go to his office. Once there he sat behind his desk, pointed to a chair. I sat down then passed the package of diamonds to him. Ten beautiful round cut diamonds dancing in the packages. He tapped them around with his finger asking in a curious way. Which I knew was more like a warning.

"Are these the real fucking Issue"?

"Does a bear shit in the woods" I replayed.

You have my word on that. "No Bullshit".

He looked at me in a respectable manner. Then he asked the question. "So, what do I want for everything"? "$10K" I said. "I'll give you $7k in cash right now" he said. I counter his offer with a how about this proposition. I'll accept the $7k you're offering. But I also want the privileges of coming into your establishment without paying the entrance fees, or for drinks for a while. He smiled said "as long as you don't abuse your privilege you are all set".

"Deal", he swiveled the chair he was sitting in opened the safe. When he swiveled back around, in his hand was a stack of bills. He counted $7k out all in big Benjamin's. Handed them right to me in money bands. There was no need for me to count the money, only the need to establish trust. I reached into my pocket and pulled out the three packages of gold rings then asked him what I can get for these. With a Wolfish grin to myself.

He smiled the Wolfish grin out loud seeing the double play. He gave me $2k more for all of them. So, in a way I still got around 10k with 9k but so much more in other ways. Upon the conclusion of our business, we walked around the club as he introduced me to ALL the working girls, then the bouncer who would be there every weekend at night. Before I left the club that day. Tony told me, that if I ever do come across anything make sure to come see him first.

From that day, until I would often go there to do business with Tony. I made my way back to my grandparent's apartment on the other side of town after that. Put most of the money in a hiding place. I spent some time watching T V with my grandfather, who enjoyed having a drink of whiskey. He would always say "You got that right" then at 8 p m I excused from his presence to go take a shower.

I dressed stylishly sprayed on some men's smell good, counted out $1K from my stash. Went to the phone called the red cab. When it arrived, I bid my grandfather goodbye. Stepping out into the Boston air I hopped in the cab.

"To the combat zone, 'I said to the driver.

Tonight, I was going to take advantage of the privilege that I had earned at "The Intermission club". I got out of the cab paid the driver walked in the door. The bouncer knew who I was the place was rocking patrons enjoying themselves buck naked hoes everywhere. So, I played Mr. Influential once I seen Tony was there. I walked up to him said hello, he asked me to accompany him as we walked around the club. He informed all that worked there that I had VIP privileges. I receive anything that I requested from drinks to sexy ladies that came along with lap dances. Then I had to go to the Champaign room with one sexy stripper where I enjoyed all the benefits that she invoked upon me. I tipped her and made my way back to the other floor. I was back into the life, so I bought a $100 worth of powdered cocaine to sniff with the ladies. Around midnight I called a cab went home you know I slept like a baby I was partied out.

Downtown Boston was now my hustling grounds. I knew so much about the city it's streets all the ins all the outs. I had numerous different places to earn a profit with so many opportunities lined up. I did not worry about burning up any one place. I would grab a name tag from a company store go in early. Walk around like someone that worked there blending in hustling at the same time. Most of the time no employee would question me, even if they did, I had the right answer sometimes I was even in the morning meeting.

Then it happened. My addiction to cocaine became a monster it took on legs of its own. Which was causing me to hustler in a matter that was not conducive to the way that I had been hustling. Felt as if I was working backwards. As shit got worse, I had to buy my get high in some of Boston's worst neighborhoods. Like Grove Hall Castle Gate & Humboldt Ave. There I was pulling up in a midnight blue Cadillac dressed up looking like an executive in a three-piece. Only I was going into a shooting gallery to get high in the company of junkies.

I knew that I stood out, but I wasn't worried about something happening to me. I was there to get high. With my years of experience in the ghetto streets I knew how to respond to my surrounding. Plus, I was spending hundreds of dollars just about every day. I was caught up in an age-old cycle caused by addiction that would cause me to over hustle taking risk that I would not normally take. I was still doing my thing, getting up early in the morning going into the city and hustling. But I had developed a somewhat serious cocaine habit that needed to be fed just about every day. So, I was now over hustling everyday stealing jewelry and brand name clothing only I was settling for pennies on the dollars.

It was a Thursday morning. I made my way downtown I decided to go into what was one of my most profitable places the jewelers building. I'm walking from floor to floor when I noticed this shop, I didn't see anyone at, or behind the counter. I could see a safe behind the counter that was slightly opened. I went into the store as quite as possible adrenaline pulsating. I stood there for a moment waiting for someone to come from the back to assist me, but no one did.

I went behind the counter reached into the open safe stole ten small gold bars, along with a gold bracelet then quickly exited. I decided to stay in the building. Thinking to myself that if by chance someone happened to notice they would assume I already left. The last place police would suspect was that I was still in the building.

I went to a bunch of other floors never back to the one where I had done my deed. Just making observations of different shops. Another shop caught my attention something about the way it looked. It was not a large shop plus there were no customers in it. When I entered, the sound of a bell announced my presence. Most of the display cases didn't have that much jeweler in them. A heavy-set man came from the back of the shop he spoke with a country accent.

"Howdy" he said, how I can help you. Game recognized game there was something about him and the shop. I worked my way into a conversation with him about certain jewelry items in the display case. We also spoke about the price of gold according to the market and all other things related. Then I asked if he had recently opened his store.

"Yup," he said he also mentioned that he was from Texas. Then I said to him, "I have a friend that's trying so sell some gold". I asked if he knew of someone that he could sell such items to. However, the only problem was that he did not have any type of I.D. Too sweeten it I said that the guy was not trying to get rich just a fair price. From the look on his face, I could tell that he was interested. Texas said that he would be interested in buying if the price was right. I told him that I would be back in about an hour then walked out.

I did not leave the building. I just went to the opposite end of the hallway like a wolf observing it prays surrounds I waited. Occasionally, I'd take a look in the direction of the shop to see if the police went rushing in. After about thirty minutes when no police arrived, I knew that I had a fence. No need to procrastinate just get on with business. When I returned, he came to the counter. I handed him five of the ten gold bars that I had grabbed. He tested them, then asked how much I wanted for them.

An ounce of gold in the 1980s was about $400 to $500 an oz. I had 4 or $5k worth. I asked for $3500 knowing that I was going to get lowballed. So, I accepted his offer of $2500. After all it was all about making the connection. It worked eventually turning into many different Thelonious sales, plus me and Tex became good friends. We snorted coke together, had different female acquaintances entertain us in the back of his store things were copasetic from that day forward.

I went to enjoy the fruits of my hustle that afternoon. I did things big Willy style. I went for lunch in the Back Bay at one of the many restaurants' social clubs on Boylston Street. I ate while socializing with the suits and skits blending right in. After eating, I went to a pay phone to call my sweetheart lady bunz. I asked her if she wanted to go out for dinner with me later tonight, she agreed.

I walked to the train station. The whole ride on the train I was deep in thought reflecting on the events of the day all the way home. I took a power nap until around seven p.m. Got up washed up dressed then cut out the apartment again. I made a stop at the florist shop on my way to Bunz house purchased a dozen roses.

I knocked on the door, Rhonda answered there I was with a dozen of roses in my hand. She was pleased so was I. Not only by how sexy she looked but she had beautiful eyes. We went upstairs to her place. I watched television as she showered and got dressed. When she finally appeared, she was in a pair of Sassoon jeans that fitted her bunz like a glove.

Into the night we drove in her car. Our destination was to the top of the Prudential Towers to dine at the Sky Walk. She parked in the Prudential garage we rode the elevator hand and hand to the top of the tower. Once seated we ordered our drinks. Looking out at Boston's skyline as I am waiting for my drink to arrive. I sit back to relish in the awesomeness of my hustling accomplishments. I felt like I was sitting on top of the world. The awesome view of the city a sexy, beautiful lady complimenting me. I could not help but to reminisce about my journey here. I was a man from Florida now with a pocket full on money looking out from one of Massachusetts tallest building. I was on top of my game in tune with the state's motto "Making it in Massachusetts". Drinks arrived then we order dinner. We toasted to it all. After the second drink we became more at ease the conversation flowed.

After dinner we went down to the ground level, walked around enjoying the many shops that Boston had to offer. Later, as we drove back to Roxbury. I suggested that we stop at club ROSCOE it was time for me to show off in the hood. Not only my style but the fine sexy lady that I had under my arm. I walked in like that guy who orders the most expensive cognac. I made some small talk around to the normal gang in there. Then told everyone drinks were on me. Everyone howled "WOOOOLF" they all cheered then we toasted to the good life.

The music was jumping we made our way to the dance floor. From the way Rhonda moved her ass it was quite evident why she was my Lady Bunz. After dancing we had a few more drinks, from out of the darkness my jones surfaced but I paid it no attention. It was lady's night the ladies were everywhere. But tonight, would not be lady's night for me I held back my player instinct.

I was there with my lady, but I wanted to experience being at the club by myself for the first time. So, I devised a plan. I told Rhonda that I had something to do in the morning that we would be leaving soon. We drove around for a while I turned on the tape player, rolled up a joint we smoked as the sound of jazz moved through the air.

The conversation was pleasing we discussed her day, then I told her about my thoughts. How I felt about her and how she makes me feel. I complimented her on how beautiful she looked then said that being with her tonight was incredibly special. My desire for the cocaine was calling but I kept it in check. I asked if she could take me to the train station she agrees. I thanked her for a wonderful night it ended with a kiss. I got out of the car said my goodnight then she drove off. Then I turned around went right the fuck back to Roxbury.

I was somewhat familiar with Roxbury I went back to the club Roscoe. As I told you it was Thursday night lady's night. The Pimps, Players, hustlers, dope dealers all would be there. I sat down ordered my usual Bacardi and coke with a twist of lime. With my drink in hand, I walked over to the juke box just standing there for a while in the neon light soaking in the scene. The music was jumping as the D J played the latest sounds. All types of ladies, tall, short, slim, thick, super fine ones. I mean broads dancing wall to wall this was the 80s the music coming through the speakers: Teddy Pendergrass, Cool and the Gang, the Whispers, the Gap Band, R&B, that funk soulful beat your known to love. It was converting into rap no or days you would also here Sugar Hill Gang, Curtis Blow, Run D M C. They were rocking crazy hard at the time as well.

I made my way back to the bar. I made a second look at the lady attending the bar. She too was fine tall, thick around the hips. Her skin was brown chocolate she walked over to where I was, asked if I wanted another drink. "Yes", I said but what I would really like is your name. "Lillian", she replied. "That is a beautiful name" I said. "By the way I'll have a Bacardi and coke with a twist of lime." When she returned with my drink, I involved her in the conversation by asking where she was from? She told me she was from the local area just working the weekend shift. But a few times out of the week she worked the evening shift. I ask if she had a male friend, she said that she did but told me it was not nothing serious. I knew what that meant. I could not hold her there long as she was working and had to go fill her obligation.

She walked away to take another order when she return, she slipped me her phone number. I walked around the club sipping my drink enjoying the show as the honeys were shaking there ass out on the dance floor. Before I left, I said goodbye to Lillian told her that I'll call in hopes we could get together sometime possibly do something amazing. She smiled hopefully I had made another female friend.

I left the club out into the night air did some walking around within the hood. You know just kicking it getting to know the mood of the people as well as the owners of all the different stores. I found it to be an interesting mixture of the culture of Blacks and Spanish culture. With the smell of all that mixture I made my way into a sub shop it was Spanish owned. The owner was cool we talked developing good understanding. I left with the fact that I would be able to return if I had something knew to sell. I caught the train and a bus back to Brookline. I did not get high that night. The next morning, I was famished it was time to eat cooking breakfast was not an option for me. But I was with Rhonda the option might present itself.

I had grown accustomed to this lifestyle but the thing that I needed was my own place. Rhonda and I had been together for two years one day she asked me if I wanted to move in with her. So, I was now living with Rhonda in Roxbury. In that same environment where all the dope, women along with everything in between. Of course, I got caught up in just about all it offered.

# EARLY HUSTLER GETS THE MONEY

Another lesson that I learned was that the earlier the better. Opportunities often presented itself in those early hours. Many employees were not at their peak levels of performance so to speak, at least until they had that proverbial second cup of coffee. Starting early always meant many of the doors were unlocked. If anyone were to be in the store during those hours, they would not have a clue. Either the cleaning maintenance crews, or employees who had no idea and do not get paid enough to question someone dressed up like me. I called it a Wolf in Sheep's clothing.

I had the skills to respond appropriately to just about anyone I would encounter. I started dressing for the type of business building I intend on hustling from. These types of situations often produced some profitable opportunities for me. I Often entered open offices only to come upon cash bags just sitting on top of desk. Or a safe unlocked money just sitting out in opened cash registers along with cash bags next to them. While casually walking I would use my Wolf like listening skills I would often hear the manager of the establishment going about their daily business. This was key since I knew they were not in the office. So, I would go to where the safe was open it up take not only any money that was in the safe but also the deposit bag(s).

Most stores especially the large ones had the usual employee entrance. That did not stop me getting in was always so easy. Once inside in order to make walking around not a problem. I would snatch up a store tag, or required store shirt, or lab coat of an employees. So, as I was making my rounds in the office or anywhere throughout the store, I could blend in. If I was confronted by someone that did work, there all I would do is say good morning and keep it moving.

I was always exuding confidence as I went about my business of hustling. My presence in those department stores were so often. That I believed that employees thought that I was a hired employee. I remember this one event it was much earlier than I usual went into Boston. With a tag pinned to my shirt I made my way downtown the department store. I went to the employees' entrance, when I pulled at the door it was open but there was no security. There were very few lights on in the store at all. I could hear cleaning machines. I made my way up the escalator to the men's department. I came upon expensive men jogging suits, so I put a blue one over the clothing I was wearing.

After I walked around looking for a leather carrying bag to fill with expensive men's clothing.  But something draws my attention in another direction my Wolf senses start tingling.  I hear woman's voices they were talking about money, so I went to investigate. In what seemed to be an office area the two female voices I heard was coming from the back of it. Someone was in training from the contents of the conversation when I looked behind the counter, I couldn't believe what I saw there had to be over 20 black cash draws with money just sitting there loaded up.

Swiftly with no hesitation like a wolf in the winter.  I went behind the counter keeping my eyes alert, glued, my ears tuned pointed up on sonic hearing mode to the conversation going on between the two women, along with everything else going on around me.  Always grabbing the large bills first, the $100's, then $50s, and then $20s from cash draw to cash draw folding wads of bills into my pockets. Next the 10s, and 5's luckily   the two extra sets of clothing I had on came in handy. Satisfied with what I had found it was time to get the fuck out of there.

Quickly, as quiet as possible down the escalators to the first floor, onto to the employees' entrance I went. But when I get there, I encounter an unarmed female security officer at the door. I wasn't worrying I did have on my employee work tag, so I just maintained my cool. Boldly I continued towards the door. When I get ready to open the door, she asks to see my employee tag? I thought that I had it on, but I must have lost it in the shuffle somewhere in the store. It was not where I had pinned it, but I wasn't going to let nothing stop me from leaving with all this money. Without saying a word, I nod then, pushed pass her onto the streets of downtown Boston acting like I didn't speak English or even understood what she said.

She called for me to stop, so I just mixed into the rush of the city people. Getting as far away from the area as possible. I could hear in the air the siren sound of the Boston police cars. So, like superman in the booth changing back to Clark Kent. I duck into one of the office building lobbies hiding in the darkness of the corner stair way. The blue jump suit that I took from the store, I rid myself of it. Putting the money in every pocket available even in my socks. I throw the clothing into the lobby trash can while exiting the building. I'm back on to the street now in a shirt with dress pants limping as if I had a bum leg. A police car comes from around the corner I knew I was in their sight as they rode slowly by looking at me before continuing on. It was time for me to get to the train station as fast as possible before another police cruiser precariously comes around the corner with a better description then the last one.

I noticed a single white young lady walking slightly ahead of me. It seemed as if she too was headed towards the train station. I called out to her pleasantly in a southern accent. She stopped then turned around. Me still in my limping act, I made my way towards her kindly asking her if she would please help me. In my best southern charm I said, "miss can you please help me I do believe that I'm lost." "I'm just visiting Boston and must have taken the wrong train." "I'm trying to get to the Mass General Hospital to visit a friend." "Can you please be so as kind tell me please what train I should catch."

I was glad when she offered to help, even happier to hear that she was heading in the same direction. I suggested that I tag along with her then she could show me what train I needed to catch. I walked as close as I could to her indulging in casual conversation as we made our way to the train station. From the corner of my eye, I noticed a police officer on foot patrol. I heard as he spoke into his walkie talkie asking for a description of the person along with what type of clothing they were wearing. I was on edge like a muthafucker, but I maintained my composer as her and I walked right by him towards the train station.

Down the tunnel onto the platform, she kindly gave me directions, then she went her way while I waited staying tight up against the wall nervously waiting for the next train. I didn't have to wait very long looking first for any sign of police before I boarded there were none around. I sat down in the furthest corner seat of the train my socks and pockets were filled with cash although I was at ease as the train began moving. I got off then hopped back on to reverse direction. Heading back onto the orange line to get back into Roxbury. Scott free with all the loot. It was still early morning by the time I got back home. I had enough to buy a car it was not even 8am.

That was the morning I went to cash out on a used mid night blue four door Cadillac. I Still had plenty of money on hand my cocaine habit was calling. I drove the Caddie back into the hood to Humboldt and Homestead where I had been getting high at the time. This was one of the many shooting galleries, so they were called, but this place I knew a guy name Bay Bro. He knew where to get what I wanted. He always took me to the spot where the cap boys were selling some of the best drugs in the area. I had satisfied my habit for the time.

But it was that habit that would be my downfall. Most of the money I was getting was going to getting high that within itself cause my hustling game major problems. That addiction and desire caused me to slip up. I was not paying attention like a wolf would senses became dulled, reactions slower. These mistakes would lead me down the road to prison. Instead of getting a house sentence, I got a Concord five. This was my first 5-year state bid. As I did my time Rhonda decided to move to Sacramento California. We continued a long distant relationship she was my support all throughout my time away. When I was released, she sent me a plane ticket to come to California. I left Boston without permission from my parole officer in doing so it meant that there was a warrant for me back in Massachusetts. I was in the wind.

# California and back to Boston

Sacramento California was different in comparison to other states I had previously lived in. The street life is street life no matter where you reside. It is basically the same and that's by "The Man's design". Although there are different animals in these woods that I had not yet encounter in all my years. The different gangs along with the gang culture was very different to me. I never understood what all the fighting and waring was about, I was not raised in gang culture. So, this did not concern me because I was from Boston. I belonged to no particular gang or set, to them I was considered neutral.

However, I was aware of the color code that the gangs adhere to, as well as the other gang politics. Being a young Black man in California you don't want to be mistaken for being with it. so as to not get mixed, Bloods wore a lot red, Crips wore blue, I respected their ideology but kept my distance.

When I got to Sacramento Rhonda had already established herself, she had a car, and was living in condo in a very pleasant neighborhood. The only thing that I needed to do was to get familiar with my new forest. So that I could get to doing what I do best hustling.

It didn't take long for me to reacclimate my way into the life. I started making good money, that along with her income enabled us to enjoy the many different opportunities that were available. Always dinning out in the finest restaurants. We added all kinds of state-of-the-art electronic devices to the condo. We had just about every kind of home necessity there was we lived very comfortable for a time.

Since I had my drug habit in check the relationship with my girl was going wonderful. As a hustler I'm always on the lookout for something profitable. Since we were living in one of Sacramento's fairly good neighborhoods. One that was surrounded by other condos so, I decided to take a stroll of the surrounding hood. That day it was California hot out, as I am making my tour through the surrounding complexes in the neighborhood. I come upon what was just one of the many pools. There I saw were all these beautiful ladies swimming and tanning in their sexy bikinis. To me this was an opportunity to try something I haven't done my stock market game.

I had some knowledge and understanding of the market. I learned how to read the daily stock market report. The next afternoon with the Wall Street Journal and a pencil in hand. I made my way to the pool area. The ladies where doing what they do swimming tanning the usual.

I sat at one of the vacant patio tables under the coolness of the umbrella sporting a pair of manly trunks. I'm going over the report, making lines in different sections of the paper. Making sure to do that with a serious look on my face as if I was making some momentous stock decision.

I didn't stay long, just long enough I thought to capture one of those ladies' attentions. I tried to make that walk down to the pool as close to the same time at least twice a week. It was the third week when I finally caught the attention of one of the lovelies. She walked up to me inquired about what it was that I was so focus on I told her to sit down let me explain.

After exchanging names one that I now present day cannot recall. she asked again what I was doing. I gave her a quick layman's course from the knowledge that I knew about stocks as well as other possible investment ideas. The conversation continued past the stock market. We started to tell each other about our lives then work professions. I led her to believe that I was a bachelor living comfortable off my investments. The next time that I saw her by the pool she asked me to sit with her then she proceeded to asked me what to do if she every decided to invest in stocks for herself. After informing her that she must remember that there's always the risk factor of losing when investing in the market. I told her she should consider that when deciding how much money she is willing to invest. I went in another direction with the conversation after that to lighten things up. Which led to laugher and smiles.

Then I asked her if she would be interested in going out with me, she said that she would think about it. After that encounter with her, I decided to stay away from the pool area for about a week. This was all a part of my game. But on serval occasions I would walk in the hiding of the condos close to the pool unnoticed to check, see if she was down by the pool at the same time. When I confirmed that she was I waited and stayed away. This created the feeling of missing out.

After the week had passed, I grabbed a bottle of Chardonnay from the cabinet along with two wine glasses then headed down to the pool. She was sitting in one of the pool chairs, I walked up to her said hello, then asked her if she would like to share a bottle of wine. She was surprised to see me then asked me where I had been.

"New York", I said

as I began pouring two glasses of wine. she asked me about New York that's when I told her about some investments I had made in the market. I told her that I made a little over $10k off my investment. I could tell she was impressed from the look on her face.

We talked for a while and drank. Then she asked me if it was possible for me to invest some money that she had saved up the next time I go to New York.

"Anything is possible" I told her

If she was serious, then the next time I see you I will have some good investments that we could go over. The following evening when I saw her, I informed her that I had been following the review of some good stock investments that could possibly result in both of us making some money. If she was interested, I told her I am heading off to New York Friday morning. If she really wants to make some money, then she should have at least $5K. I am investing $5k and if all goes right her $5K should bring her a very profitable return on her investment.

I didn't want to seem like that was my only reason for talking with her. I quickly changed the subject taking it in another direction. Things began to flow as the wine took it to a more pleasurable direction. I could tell that she started feeling some kind of way as the evening turned into night. It was still warm outside from the long California sun. she stood up removed her sun dress which reviled what was a sexy swimsuit then she got into the Jacuzzi holding her hand out as an invitation to me. I climbed in between kisses touching her we then finished the bottle of wine off.

The moment was getting hot she put her hand down my swimming trunks began massaging my dick it became hard. I returned the pleasure as I pulled her bottom bikini to the side with my index finger I began playing with her clit, she became aroused. I remover her bottom bikini so she could mount my erected dick. From the moans that she made her body was pleased with ever inch that I offered. It didn't take but a few minutes for her to come and in the excitement of it all I busted into her hot pussy.

We then relaxed in the warm bubbles of the jacuzzi. I informed her that I would be going to New York with a plan to invest then be back in two days. she said that she'll have the $5000 to invest and to call her before I leave. After getting her phone number I went back to my condo with a wolfish grin it was a very goodnight.

I spent the next two days hustling items from the mall across the street where we lived. It was an easy hustle for me ever since that day I walked into that department store back East. I now knew the stores designs, without stopping I headed straight to the back of the warehouse. I picked up a box that said Sony. Inside was a stereo system I placed it on a dolly then rolled it right out the store. It became so easy this was my money-making hustle. I took two more from that store sold them in the next two days. Sold one to my dealer then the another to someone else.

After the two days had gone by, I dressed in my businessman outfit to project the image called her told her my flight to New York was schedule to leave at six pm. She told me that she had the $5k I was to meet her at the pool around 4pm. She was waiting for me in the pool area when I arrived. I sat down informed her of my intentional stock picks. After convincing her that I was on the right track she handed me the $5K along with a good luck kiss. I informed her that I'll see her in two days.

Knowing damn well there was no trip to New York. Instead, I went to my dealer it was time to get this jones satisfied. I was flying high and thought I was ahead of the game. I sat in the smoke house getting high amongst the other smokers of coke and Newport's. After I left with no intention of hustling. Instead, I decided to investigate other potential possibilities of the female kind. I was out and about fox hunting throughout the hood when this associate that I had done a few hustles with pulled up in a car. He told me that he was on his way to do a Heist that he had set up. He asked me if I would assist him.

I saw no harm in helping another man in the game all I had to do was be the lookout guy. I was still in my high zone when he pulled up into this apartment complex. I usual only work businesses. He knew that so I thought that he was just going to grab something although I was too high to realize this was the heist. I waited out in the car outside as he went to do what he had planned. In a few minutes he returned with a few items, put them into the trunk of the car then ask me to watch he'll be right back. There I was waiting in a car with stolen household items waiting for him to return.

Someone saw what was going on then called the police. Him and I were arrested on the spot the rest was history. I got five years for breaking and entering. Being that I had an out of state warrant hold on me from Massachusetts I had to do that time at a maximum prison. Pelican Bay I did two years on that five and was expedited back to Boston.

I did my time reading and studying learning all that I could if there were classes being offered, I was first in line to sign up. I was finally cleaned up I went to AA and NA along with other related classes. The dictionary and thesaurus were my companions. I worked out with the weights. I also became an advent chess player the game of a thinking man.

One night as my cellie (cell mate) and I were playing chess he asked me what my plans were once I am released. I told him about the hustles I was doing that I didn't have a real plan just to go back to Boston then get back into the life. He pulled a folder from his property produced photos of the life he had lived when he was out there in the real world. I was impressed with his past then he proceeded to give me the game on how he was able to live the way that he did not working a nine to five job.

I listened soaking up the OG's game waiting to ask questions after that conversation. I knew that I had been giving something rare. It was up to me to do with information as I please but respect the knowledge. I didn't make a turn around, but I had to return to the same people and environment that I wanted to avoid. Rhonda had moved on she was no longer living in the hood. As far as her and me getting back together it wasn't going to happen. There was no going back. I understood, but her mother said that I could rent one of the rooms on the second floor of the house that she purchased in the city Lynn, Mass. There was an old saying from the 1940's. "Lynn, Lynn city of sin…You never come out the same way you came in".

This would prove to be true resulting in a difficult time for me. Not only was there a drug dealer living on the first floor, but the third floor was a smoking galley. I tried to avoid that road, but it was people, places, and things and I got caught up in it all over again. I was doing a lot of creeping those days going in the warehouses of stores, or in the back taking items of value. Sometimes I would get lucky, someone would leave their purse on the table in the brake room, or left their locker unlocked. I would take the cash only. No place was safe from me. I was like a rabid Wolf hunting around the woods with reckless abandon.

I went into a business technology building during working hours scoped the place out. Then at night when they were closed, the cleaning crew was usually there. I would creep in through my previously found access to take computers. I would hide them outside to be picked up later with a partner. I would take anything of value or what I thought I could sell. There was no commonality to what I was doing. No method to my madness. I was making good money my rent was always paid and I wasn't selling everything that I took. I maintain the image of a man of extremely good means my living conditions always state of the art. Even though the monkey of addiction was still on my back.

One night as I was upstairs getting high with the rest of smokers. This lady who was up there often I would notice looking at me. She said to me that I was out of my element. That I shouldn't be up here smoking, told me that every time she saw me, I was clean. My clothing was brand name, I always had money, was wearing expensive jewelry. She couldn't understand it.

It registered but, what she said didn't sink in. As the years went by, and it was some years. I remembered what that woman said that day. You see when you are getting high you tend to lose yourself as well as time. I realized I was getting tired with the bullshit that getting high brought. The character of people around well most of them any way was slimy. Even though I did what would be considered bad things and got high like they did. I was always true to the game. I never tried to beat or set up the same people that were in the streets trying to make a dollar like I was. That was why I didn't fit in that world their world had no code. They say there is honor amongst thieves. But as I looked around there was no thieves, I only seen smokers chasing the ghost of addiction. This wasn't the same forest.

I don't know if that was the force behind me making the change, or maybe I just grew out of it. But once I stop getting high my thinking cleared up. My hustling changed for the best. I no longer needed to spend my cash on drugs and frivolous things. I was now able to save up, stack my paper, bag my chippers! I had books on a self that was really a safe it stayed full just like big Tony's at the strip club used to be.

While I always kept at least a few thousand in my pocket every day. Letting go of the drugs was the only thing that saved me. I knew so many other players and hustlers of that time that went down that road to never return. As for this Alpha I was back in the game proper.

# GAME CHANGER

It was a Thursday night when I met Marianna. What started off as just another day for me in the hustler game I was out and about, in and out of businesses doing my thing. Looking for that opportunity. It didn't take long for me to get my hands on two credit cards. After getting those I went to Radio Shack to purchase certain items on my list of things that people I knew had requested. The barter system was one of the ways you got money from the credit cards back then. I was always aware of the latest electronics as well as technologies. If it was coming out, I had it for sale before anyone. So, I purchased a lab top using two credit cards splitting the payment in half between the two cards. Then I went to another store to purchased other high-tech items that were on the list.

I drove back to Lynn to sell each item to their perspective customers. Now I had cash in my pocket. I was hungry and thirsty, since I was in Lynn, I headed to Charlie Chan's a Chinese food restaurant that served good drinks located on Union Street. This location was considering the hood a local hang out spot. Where thug's, drugs, and just about anything one wanted one can get.

I parked my white Lincoln continental in front of the place stepped out like I was the Mack of the year then went in. I was dressed to impress as always. I made my presence known as I greeted those that I knew while I made my way to the bar. I placed my order for food along with a drink rum and coke with a twist of lime. I dropped a few coins in the slot of the jukebox played a few songs. when it was time to pay, I used one of the credit cards I knew that I could get cash back from the card at the restaurant. Excuse me I said to the female bar tender can I get some cash back from my credit card the limit is $500 she said.

I paid for the meal and the drink then got my $500 cash back. Weeks later that same female bar maid worked with me after she told me that she knew I was using swiped cards. I was enjoying the moment. I found a new insider for the hustle. I was soaking it all in when my eyes caught the attention of one of the hood flowers looking at me. It had to be me style in the way I was dressed. I was the only man at the bar dressed in a business suit and tie.

She nodded at me she stood up and came over to sit next to me. What's your name she asked me after the introduction we got better acquainted over a few drinks. I shared my Chinese food with her. She was Cuban and worked as a nurse. When she asked me what I did for a living I was honest.

I said, "I'm a HUSTLER".

Thinking back, I don't think she knew what that was at the time.

The first day was one of getting to know each other before the club closed, I asked her if she could give me a ride at the end of the night, I left my ride at the crib on purpose. We made plans to see each other again. As time went by, we got more acquainted with each other grew closer. She would often come to my apartment after her work to pick me up. Then we would go to our spot for drinks at the restaurant's bar on Union Street.

One night she came to pick me up. Told her to hop in my ride. I offered to take her to a fine dining restaurant. I would pay for everything with credit cards I had snatched earlier that day. After dinner we went to a club to dance and drank the night away. It was getting closer to closing time so, I suggested that we leave before the traffic gets busy. As were driving back she asked if it would be alright to go to my place. We arrived at my place then make or way up the stairs. For a lady of 52 she was dam sexy and could fuck I had my hands filled with this one. I had to put work in that serious work her pussy game was no joke.

At night as we laid in the bed you could hear the knocks coming from downstairs from buyers looking for cocaine from the dealer that lived on the first floor. Then after buying what they wanted they made their way up the stairs to the third floor to get high. The next morning, I hit it again before she made her way home. I tried to fuck her ankles loose. After fucking her for the third time she asked me if I wanted to come to live with her in Salem.

I accepted and moved in. It was not as comfortable as I would have wanted it to be. But at least people were not buying dope acting crazy all times of the night. The problem isn't from her it was coming from her asshole son. I did my best to get along with him. I even tried to school him in the way of the game, but he was fifteen years old and stupid. Him and I struggled from time to time. He was too far gone within himself and stubborn to be taught the parts of the game that he needed to be successful in this life. This would make me think. What exactly I had to understand, or what it was that I needed to do in order to get to where it was that I needed to get.

But what really threw me for a lope was. I thought I was getting out and away from the drug environment only to learn later that she was also smoking coke. She did have a job I would take her to work in her SUV. Allowing me to keep my car parked and clean. The only requirement that she had was that I had to be there with a bottle of Rum when I picked her up after her shift. We lived in a good area of Salem. I just needed to get to know how to find my way around. I remember this one afternoon I had to pick her son up from school because he had got into some kind of trouble. To my surprise I was able to get in the school with no problem. As I was making my way down the hallways, I notice serval classrooms doors open the classrooms where unoccupied the teachers along with the students I think were at lunch.

I was going to take the money along with credit cards at first out of the teacher purse under the desk. But then my 6th sense kicked into what would be a onetime opportunity. I noticed that there had to be six maybe seven credit cards. I left the money took two of the six credit cards from the back end. Leaving the one on top there. I went in three other classrooms did the same thing. I left that school with six credit cards. The first thing I did was to fill up the tank along with the most expensive car wash.

I had I found my new hustle, but then I remember that conversation that I had with the OG in prison back in California don't disrespect the knowledge by over doing it. Only I was going to take it to another level. I was on a road, and I wasn't going to turn around anytime soon. Using other people credit cards to get just about anything that I wanted. From the car wash/ gas station I was off to the mall. I bought me a $2500 diamond ring that was on sale. My next purchase was clothing. This is where I put my own thought to it instead of using the same card for each purchase once I used the card it went to the back of the card pile. I did this with every purchase I used one of the other cards. Back then without suspicious activity the cards would just run up.

I bought my clothing with another card. came to a little over $200 that was a small purchase. On to the next store I had to get that newest invention at the time a DVD player as well as DVDs the price $500 plus it ran right up no problems.

It was time for lunch at Joe's. I ordered a Filet Mignon baked potato, spinach with sour cream. Always the best when I found good hustle because I was hungry. Everything paired with a great wine. Enough time had gone by without it being used so I bought a 50″ screen TV. I picked up a few bottles of liquor from the liquor store. Then I closed the day out at Stop and Shop shopping for all name brand groceries. When I checked out it came to over $500 in groceries. On my way back home, I stop to once again to refuel get another car wash for good measure. As I was putting away all the things that I had bought. I thought to myself I couldn't wait until tomorrow to do it again. I made my way to pick up my Cuban lady from work. Of course, I had her bottle of rum, but it was top self. We picked up something to eat to bring back home. When she walked into the pad, I could see the look of surprise and appreciation on her face. When she saw the new 50-inch flat screen TV accompany with an DVD player in the living room. Along with a fridge full of a months' worth of the best food you can buy.

She took a shower and changed into something comfortable. I turned on the TV put one of the movies in the DVD and set up for dinner. The beginning of our relationship went good until, the day I went back to smoking cocaine. It seemed like I just couldn't get away from cocaine, and I fell into the drug trap again. I was still doing what I had been doing but using drugs didn't go along with where I wanted to go. The years went by and within those years I did some lock up time. Her and I communicated by letters and phone calls. Marianne did her part by taking care of business. I was never in need of anything during those years. It was only right to retune to her when I got released. By then Marianna moved to Lynn. She was still getting high, but I was determined to never use again. So as time went, and I got my feet under myself we drifted apart just going in deferent directions of life.

I had two new vices to replace getting high. One was the trill of being able to get in and out of places I had no business being in without getting caught. The second vice was me being able to purchase just about anything I wanted with the money or credit cards that I got from going in those places. Having money in my pocket enjoying some of the finest things that life had to offer. That adrenaline rush I got was the only drug that would satisfy or offset the drug habit. I was hooked bad.

Now that I had control of my drug usage it was time to make some money. Now that my mind was clear I remember how I was able to get into places to do what I do. But that suddenly seemed like short money. It was time for me to resurrect the Wolf, this time the real alpha that separates me from the reset of the pack. I was stepping in a whole new light. When I was sober. My attire was still acceptable to do what was needed. I was fresh clean cut looking like a million bucks.

I walked into this jewelry store, overheard the person working there talking about how the replica of lady Dianne's wedding ring was beautiful. The stones were not real but only a jeweler could tell. When I saw it I had to have it. I walked around waiting for the right moment. The guy that had shown the ring to the customers was busy trying to sell them something else. Instead of putting the ring back in the safe. He put it under the counter and continued trying to make a sale. He went around to the other side of the store to show the customers something else. Putting even further away.

As they were busy talking. You could tell he was on the verge of a sale. He was locked in trying to make it happen. This was a perfect time to go into alpha mode test my reflexes. I made my move it would be risky, but I thought I was the fastest man on the planet. I made a quick observation it was go time. With the quick fast it was mine it was mine.

I didn't even stay in the store immediately I left. I gave that ring to my Cuban lady who in turn sold it for less than what it was worth for cocaine. She then tried to sell me some bull shit excuse. About how the guy said she could buy it back. But now that he had it, he was not going to sell it back to her. She wanted me to go see the guy. I told her I didn't have no time for that jive ass bullshit anymore. I was not about the cost of the ring for me it was the thrill of being back in rare form anyway. Plus, I was about to drop her ass like the bad habit I left behind already. I knew it was time for me to find another lady.

I had supplied the apartment with everything that one needed to be comfortable. We even had two cats they were best. But we were living in the darkness, my Cuban lady didn't want the lights on during the day. When my day of hustling was over, I would spend most of my evening on the front pouch, or out-front detailing my car. It was one of those moments that I met the lady that I'm still with.

I was sitting on the pouch looking out across the street. There she was this lady of beauty I stood up. I had to go introduce myself, I was compelled to go talk to her. But she had disappeared somehow by the time I got across the street she was gone in the wind. However, days later I saw her again this time I kept an eye on her. "Excuse me" I said "I don't have much time, but can I please have your name and phone number. My jedi mind tricks were always up to par. Her name was Available no just kidding. Her name was Anya. Anya was no taller than 5' 5". No more than 100 lbs. Dressed like a businesswoman I was drawn to her. She gave me her information and we cordially parted ways. Turned out we had something in common have in common. We both were in an unhappy relationship. We were both on the verge of separation but not from a sex affair. She lived around the corner from where I was living that made it much more convenient for the two of us to see one another.

Anya brought balance to my life she would often bring me complete home cooked meals when my wife was at work. As my wife Marianna had stopped cooking. She was more concerned with getting high or drinking a bottle of rum. When I went over to Anya's place, I didn't have to worry about anything my mind was at ease. But even though I was at ease at her place but for me the place needed an upgrade. She was a single parent, and I understood the pressure she never asked me for anything.

I had to test her sincerity towards the relationship before I would go any further. One day during a conversation I asked her to buy me a cell phone so that her and I could communicate. The following week I met her at our usual meeting place the backyard over by the garage where I was living. That was when she gave me a brand-new NOKIA phone. I knew along with those meals that she was the lady for me. I decided what I needed to do.

We began dating more on a serious note going out to eat at some of Massachusetts finest establishments up and down route one in Saugus. I must say that all throughout our relationship she had no idea about the way I was supporting the activities and lifestyle that I was living. In the hood dwellers thought I was another drug dealer. I had a personal barber, the clothing I wore was from some of the finest clothing stores in Boston. Men's clothing that was tailored to fit. I sported all sorts of jewelry gold chains, bracelets semi-precious stone rings. I drove around in a white four door Lincoln Continental that was always waxed and cleaned inside, out. Always had a stack of money in my pocket.

I still was dealing with my wife with her addiction. She had become too deep into using. When her and I was together at a club she wouldn't listen to my advice. When I had asked her to slow down her drinking? She would take back-to-back double shots. Getting super drunk which lead her to start acting belligerent, and out of hand. I did not want to be a part of this shit show anymore.

But when I was in the company of Anya life was more in line with what I wanted. As time went by and the more time together. I knew that being with her was what I needed. Eventually it happened. I made the decision it was time for me to make that necessary change. I had a conversation with Anya. I explained to her that I was tired with the current relation with my wife and that I was ready to leave my wife. I asked to move in with her she said yes, a few days later when Marianna was at work I moved out from my current location. Leaving her everything that I had put in the house knowing I could get it all again. I just wanted to get out I took some of my clothing and jewelry along since I needed them for hustling. They were like my tools of the game.

I was true to the game now. I knew that I would get those items along with much more now that I was a happy man. I set out to give my new lady the best life that she and I could live.

I was a credit card wizard at this point. It was back to the hustle after settling into my new surroundings. But there was a hospital a couple of blocks down the street that would be my next place of interest. Getting in the hospital was no problem as always, I went there early in the morning before seven. I spent hours casing out the place.

I returned the next day to get everything that I needed in order to chaptalize in putting my plan to work. The first thing that I needed was a white lab coat, along with a stethoscope and name tag. I was able to grab those items easily. Once I looked like a doctor. We went through office after office without even a slight nod from anyone.  I put the white lab on and the stethoscope around my neck then walked out of the hospital. The next morning, I was up early showered, dressed like the other doctors that I had seen in the hospital the day before. I left out the house before seven I drove to the hospital, parked my car in the hospital parking lot. I unlocked the trunk of the car retrieved the doctor gear then put it on quick as Clark Kent in the booth.  I was dressed in a white lab coat put the gold pen and pencil in the front pocket along with the stethoscope around the back of my neck. I picked up a clip board off the car seat put it under my arm. Then locked the car door and made my way to the hospital. Once in the hospital I began making my rounds. I came upon what was the hospital library.  I went in to do my own studying. I overheard a conversation going on between doctors and nurses as they discussed medical terminology. Like always I retained some basic medical information. Then I walked out of the library returned to searching for opportunity.

I walked from floor to floor until I saw what I was looking for, an unoccupied office. I went in looked around until I found a purse. Inside the purse I remove the wallet took two credit cards from the back of what looked to be six or more cards. Replaced the wallet putting the purse in the location in which I remember it being then left the office. I continued my quest for more credit cards inside another unoccupied office. when I finally left the hospital, I had accumulated six credit cards. Back in my car I drove out of the parking lot I knew where I was heading the Peabody mall.

I parked in the mall parking lot and went into the mall. It was time for me to reestablish what I had once had. I went to three different stores I purchased two TV's a 50" flat screen and a 36". Two DVD players, all the latest movies. I called Anya asked her size in clothing and shoes. I proceeded to spend a thousand on some things nice for her. That was enough shopping at that mall for the time.

There was another mall a few blocks away. So, I drove to that mall went inside to purchase some jewelry a gold necklace with a diamond shaped heart piece for Anya. From there I continue shopping by the time I was finished my car was filled with all types of item tons of bags. I never kept a receipt. It was lunch time for me Chinese food and a warm Brandy with a pot of warm tea sounded nice.

I went to Kowloon I sat at the bar and settled in I was ready to order. I'll have the boneless ribs, with general Tso's chicken, pork fried rice. From the bar I'll have two fingers of King Louis the Xlll Cognac. Life was good after chowing down that delicious meal. I gave the bar tender one of the credit cards to pay for my tab while I sipped the last of my cognac. The card was accepted I signed the receipt slip polish off my Cognac then walked out. I sat in my car satisfied deciding my next move was the grocery shopping. I filled up the basket there so I could stock my new house. After that I ended my day with a fill up, and a car wash. I left the car wash and headed to what was now as much as my home as Anya's.

I parked in the front of the house. Removed everything that I had purchased into the house. I put the groceries away in the kitchen. Then set up the TVs and DVD player. One in the bedroom, the other in the living room. When Anya returned home from work, she was happy to see all the new things in the house. I presented her with the gold neckless. As I'm placing it around her neck, I received a warm kiss.

That would not be the last time hustling at that hospital. I remember serval times I found hundreds of dollars in lab coat pockets. Hustling there was very profitable, it was also a very interesting venture. As I would often play the role of a doctor. I didn't do any serious doctoring. I just tended to a patient lying in the bed in the emergency room waiting to be seen once. I took their vitals then made a diagnosis type of recommendation. After I told them another attendant would be in soon to give them some fluids. Well anyway that following morning I escorted my Anya to the train station, we caught the train into downtown Boston once there her and I had breakfast.

After breakfast we walked to her job. I kissed her on the lips in the lobby watched her as she walked to the elevator. I was already downtown, so I used the credit cards until they were rejected. One by one I drop them in certain locations throughout the city streets. Hoping that someone would pick them up and attempt to use them making it their problem. Since I was already downtown might as well make the best of the early time.

It wasn't long before I made my decision on another building downtown. I went in the skyscraper like my usual wolfish way blending in like the morning employees. Before folks could get their coffee and breakfast, I did my thing and was on the train back home before noon.

I drove to the liquor store purchased a bottle of E& J the drink of my barber. I drove serval blocks to the barber shop to socialize, and to get a haircut. I asked my personal Barber for a cup he tapped the bottle top. We sipped a little E&J while he cut, and we kicked the game for a few minutes. Happy with life it seemed like a Wolf had the run of the forest again. For many a moon I would be able to do what I did after that. Right up until technology changed and the world started putting all these cameras up. But I remember sitting there telling my barber as I sat in the chair getting cut as well as getting my lines tightened up;

**"Pimps, players and hustlers were just some of the scholar's teaching in the school that I attended. It would be in the city streets where I would practice my lessons. I graduated my degree in Reagan era Hustlenomics. It wasn't easy out there in the streets with all its challenges, and complication. But I was determined to maintain my position on the road that I had selected. When an Alpha is the most skilled hunter in the pack. Sometimes it is essential for him to hunt alone, if the pack is going to eat at all. I Always brought enough back for the pack I was with."**

**I told the barber, "You see. There were rules that had to be followed in order to be successful in the game. I respected the rules but of them all I would practice and hold this one true: "To always be true to the game and the game will be true to you. I am Jimmy Boulders, one of the Original Wolves. I was true to the "Hustler game" and this was my story.**

Made in the USA
Middletown, DE
31 March 2022

63413907R00154